Step-by-Step
Model Drawing

Step-by-Step Model Drawing

Solving Word Problems the Singapore Way

Char Forsten

Crystal Springs
SDE BOOKS

A division of Staff Development for Educators
Peterborough, New Hampshire

Published by Crystal Springs Books
A division of Staff Development for Educators (SDE)
10 Sharon Road, PO Box 500
Peterborough, NH 03458
1-800-321-0401
www.SDE.com/crystalsprings

Published 2010
Printed in the United States of America
20 19 18 17 16   7 8 9 10 11

ISBN: 978-1-934026-96-0

Library of Congress Cataloging-in-Publication Data

Forsten, Char, 1948-
    Step-by-step model drawing : solving word problems the Singapore
way / Char Forsten.
        p. cm.
    Includes bibliographical references and index.
    ISBN 978-1-934026-96-0
    1. Problem solving—Study and teaching (Elementary)—Singapore.
2. Word problems (Mathematics)—Study and teaching (Elementary)—
Singapore. 3. Mathematics—Study and teaching (Elementary)—United
States. I. Title.

    QA63.F67 2010
    510'.76—dc22

                                                        2009037733

Art Director and Designer: Jill Shaffer
Production Coordinator: Deborah Fredericks
Illustrator: Jill Shaffer

To Jim Grant, with thanks once again for introducing me to Singapore's Primary Mathematics Curriculum and materials in the 1990s, and to my colleagues and friends—Anni, Ban Har, Catherine, Jana, Lorraine, and Sandy—who share a passion for teaching mathematics. Their contributions and our many discussions have helped make SDE's approach to teaching model drawing to American students even more effective.

Contents

Acknowledgments

I would like to acknowledge and thank:

Sharon Smith, whose role has once again extended beyond that of editor. Her vision and guidance have made this book what it is—an invaluable resource that will help teachers and students improve their understanding of mathematics and their capacity to solve word problems.

Jill Shaffer, whose book design brings clarity to the model-drawing process.

Deb Fredericks, whose work in juggling all the pieces of the production process was invaluable in turning this book into a reality.

Other Singapore-math trainers and teachers here in the United States who have become valued friends and colleagues.

Jeffery and Dawn Thomas of SingaporeMath.com, whose friendship and support help us at Staff Development for Educators to continue our mission to help educators understand and use Singapore's highly effective math strategies.

Duriya Assis of Marshall Cavendish, whose friendship and guidance I value.

Everyone at SDE. The collective support of the entire staff makes it possible to execute our mission of helping all children to learn.

Singapore educators, whose methods—especially the model-drawing approach—help us guide students to truly understand the word problems they are solving and, literally, to draw conclusions.

An Introduction to Model Drawing

A FEW YEARS have passed since a colleague and I coauthored the book *8-Step Model Drawing*. After that book came out, I made a second trip to Singapore to spend time in classrooms and to learn more about how math is taught there. I spoke firsthand with Dr. Yeap Ban Har, a recognized and highly respected expert in all areas of Singapore's mathematics curriculum. I also had the opportunity during that trip to work with numerous educators and students in Singapore, further deepening my understanding of what has made Singapore's students so successful. What I learned, and continue to learn, is how to maximize student understanding through use of the model method. As I integrated this deeper appreciation into the training I do, I realized it was time to include it in a new book.

Part of what was reinforced for me in this latest visit to Singapore was the way in which model drawing trains students to think analytically, providing an important transition between the concrete and the abstract (the algorithm). This is something that we have been largely missing in the U.S., and as I have worked with teachers to implement the model-drawing approach in this country, I have been struck by the excitement with which both teachers and students respond. Model drawing is a powerful strategy that helps students truly understand the word problems they are solving. I want to share with you an introduction to the process that has had such a strong impact on teachers and students across the country.

Why Step-by-Step Model Drawing?

When students learn model drawing, they need to master two separate stages. First they learn the *process* or how to use model drawing to solve word problems; then they learn how to *apply* that process independently when solving word problems. Teachers in the United States have found that using Singapore's model-drawing approach dramatically increases student success in this country. But we have added another element to the model-drawing process, and that is the step-by-step approach. Brain research tells us that it helps students to chunk information when they are learning new material. Word problems require that students have the skills to read, understand, strategize, compute, and check their work. That's a lot of skills! Following a consistent step-by-step approach—and providing explicit, guided instruction in the beginning—can help our students organize their thoughts and make the problem-solving task manageable.

Let's begin in the same way you would begin with your students: by learning the steps. The ones I use in this book (see page 3) differ from those in *8-Step Model*

Drawing. Of course, you might prefer to continue with those eight steps, and that is fine. What matters, and what I have found in my work with teachers and students throughout the United States, is that most students in the U.S. benefit from *some form* of an organized, step-by-step approach to learning how to read and translate word problems into models.

The biggest difference between the steps used in *8-Step Model Drawing* and those used in this book is in the second step: before starting to solve the problem, students rewrite the question as a sentence, leaving a space for the answer. Teachers from around the country contacted me to share this change, which had made a big difference for their students. I tried it and definitely agreed with them. When students focus on the question early on, it strengthens their understanding of the problem and helps guide their thinking and modeling. However, if you prefer to have students wait until the end to write the answer in a sentence, then just skip that step.

Note that the first goal in this process is for students to learn how to use the model. For that reason, I have been consistent throughout this book with the placement of information in the model. This frees students to focus on the content of the problem and not on where to put information. With consistent practice, students develop automaticity with the model method.

Once students are automatically using the model, you may find they will ask if they can show the information differently. For example, as they progress, they may prefer to show the totals for a certain problem with a brace above or below the unit bar—not always to the right, as I show in this book. When students reach this stage, it is great! The end goal of model drawing is to build a pictorial bridge to abstract thinking. The steps are like training wheels. Eventually, when students have acquired an understanding of how to read and solve word problems, they won't need to follow steps.

Having said that, it's important to point out that one step can still be highly differentiated even when students are first learning the structure of model drawing. Any time students are computing, they should be encouraged to find the answer using different methods. This should never stop. When students share different ways to arrive at a correct answer, they not only strengthen their individual number sense but they also learn from each other.

Teaching Through Guided Practice

In the guided-practice section of this book, you will find twenty-seven model-drawing problems completely illustrated and explained. I have included specific examples of different types of word problems, along with questions and suggested dialogue that demonstrate how you might guide students through the step-by-step approach. But at this point I would like to suggest a few additional ideas that you might find helpful as you begin teaching this strategy.

Step-by-Step Model Drawing

1. Read the entire problem.

2. Rewrite the question in sentence form, leaving a space for the answer.

3. Determine **who** and/or **what** is involved in the problem.

4. Draw the unit bar(s).

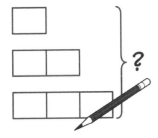

5. Chunk the problem, **adjust** the unit bars, and fill in the **question mark**.

6. Correctly **compute** and solve the problem.

7. Write the answer in the sentence, and make sure the answer makes **sense**.

An Introduction to Model Drawing

When you first introduce model drawing to your students, I would urge you to begin the process in each lesson by reflectively reading the problem. This means that you read the problem without reading the numbers. For example, suppose a problem states, "Carrie spent $12 on a book and $5 on lunch. How much total money did she spend?" Reflective reading would sound like this: "Carrie spent some money on a book. She also spent money to buy lunch. How much total

Tips for Teaching Model Drawing

■ Provide graph paper. Students who have difficulty with spacing and the alignment of numbers can benefit from using graph paper—or photocopies of the grid on page 129—for their model drawing.

■ Help with alignment. Turning lined paper sideways helps students draw unit bars. Or you can follow the example of teacher and presenter Jana Hazekamp, who suggests drawing a vertical starting line when working with more than one variable in a problem. This helps everyone line up their unit bars.

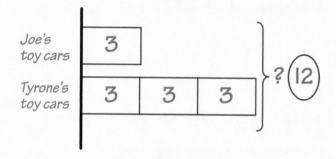

■ Have students work with model-drawing notebooks. Use each left-hand page for a problem and the model that illustrates that problem. Use the corresponding right-hand page to show the computation or work.

■ Save yourself time. Teacher and presenter Catherine Kuhns, for example, takes the idea of the model-drawing notebook one step further. She finds or creates a daily word problem. Then she types and prints the problems, cuts them into individual strips, and asks students to use glue sticks to put them in their model-drawing notebooks. Other teachers use computer programs to create labels with one problem on each label. Students get to peel and solve!

■ Ask your class not to refer to the paper on which they show their work as "scrap paper"; it's too important to be considered "scrap"! One teacher I met asks her students to call those sheets "proof papers." (In Singapore, they refer to the sheets on which they work out problems as "workings.")

■ Create your own word problems. My colleague Anni Stipek says, "A problem a day means the learning will stay!" We know that, to truly solidify understanding, most students benefit from solving additional problems that are similar to ones they have just worked with. To create your own word problems, start with the problems in the independent-practice section and change the names, numbers, circumstances, or questions. Just be certain that a word problem does not require students to call on skills, concepts, or vocabulary you have not yet introduced.

■ If some of your students have motor-skill difficulties, you might have them make a tent instead of the curly brace when drawing the models.

■ Work backward! Once students have learned and practiced a variety of problems, create a solution for any model-drawing problem. Give this solution to the class and ask each student to write a problem for the solution.

money did she spend?" Students are better able to visualize the problem without the numbers interfering with their thoughts. After you've read the problem reflectively, return and read it again, this time including the numerical information.

I would also encourage you to read the punctuation marks! When you read the question, it should sound something like this: "Carrie spent $12 on a book and $5 on lunch. Period. Stop! How much total money did she spend? Question mark. Stop." By doing this, you will help students learn to read word problems carefully, and you will also help them to internalize their understanding of punctuation.

Another practice many teachers find helpful is to have students put a check-mark over each number as they add it to the model. Also, have them put a slash after each sentence to show they have finished adding that information to the model. As adults, many of us keep lists and feel rewarded as we check off what we've completed. Students love to do this, too!

These are all good ways to begin working with each problem. Once you and your students have solved the problem, you can do even more. You can extend student thinking and computation skills and get maximum mileage from the session if you "milk the problem for all it's worth." Following the example of the questions under that heading in the guided-practice section of this book, ask additional questions that can be solved using the same model. Also, ask students to write their own questions related to the original problem. This activity is especially beneficial as a homework assignment.

One goal of using model drawing is to develop algebraic thinking, so Problems 26 and 27 in the guided-practice section show how to make that connection. Both of these problems are solved first through the model approach and then algebraically. These examples, and the final problems in the independent-practice section, demonstrate how to clearly link the pictorial and abstract stages of problem solving.

Following Up with Independent Practice

Once you have provided direct, interactive instruction using the model-drawing process, it's time for your students to practice what they've learned. Remember: practice makes permanent! The independent-practice section of this book provides forty-three practice problems ready for you to copy and hand out to students; illustrated solutions appear in the back of the book. As in the first section, I have included problems at several levels for addition, subtraction, multiplication, division, mixed operations, fractions, decimals, ratio, rate, percentage, and a bridge to algebra.

I'd like to offer a very important suggestion here, which is that you solve each problem yourself before assigning it to students or guiding them through the process. Practice is good for teachers, too!

Understanding What Comes Before Model Drawing

Model drawing is an important part of the math curriculum in Singapore, but it is far from the *only* strategy used there. As you begin introducing model drawing to your students, it is helpful to know how it fits into the broader mathematics program in Singapore. You may find that your students would also benefit from some of Singapore's other strategies. (Also, please note that model drawing is not intended as a replacement for all of the other approaches—Guess and Check, Look for Patterns, and so on—that are commonly taught in both Singapore and the United States. Those strategies are important, and they're effective. Model drawing, however, can give your students an extremely valuable problem-solving tool to add to the more familiar approaches.)

In Singapore, classroom instruction is in English, starting in kindergarten. Since most students are English-language learners, their introduction to problem solving is through an oral-language approach called "Look and Talks," often based on nursery rhymes and fairy tales. First, students learn the rhymes or stories, and then they explore related illustrations to practice skills they are learning, such as counting, grouping, measuring, subitizing, and creating math stories. My colleague Torri Richards and I wrote a book incorporating this method of understanding early math concepts; it's titled *Math Talk*.

In first grade, in Singapore's Primary Mathematics Curriculum, the first semester focuses on students learning and understanding number bonds to ten. (In the U.S., we refer to these as "fact families.") Problem-solving activities at this stage invite students to create number-bond stories, matching number bonds to pictures or illustrations. As students learn number bonds and number sentences, the numbers are always presented in context. One example would be this number-bond story for six:

A student might make up a number-bond story such as this: "I have a total of 6 toys. 2 of them are blocks and 4 of them are dolls."

After they make up their own number-bond stories, students are introduced to word problems—and to strengthen student understanding, each word problem includes actual illustrations of the objects in the problem. Students also use manipulatives, such as tiles, to "act out" a problem. For the above number-bond story, students would begin with two tiles that represent the blocks. Then they would add four more tiles representing the dolls. The tiles represent the objects in the word problem.

Fitting Model Drawing into the Learning Continuum

Once students are ready to move on to drawing models, they begin to work with the discrete method of model drawing. Working with small numbers, students draw one square to represent each object in the problem. This reinforces their understanding of one-to-one correspondence. Following up on the example, a student working with the discrete model would first draw two squares to represent the blocks and then draw four more squares to stand for the dolls. The student has moved from using manipulatives to using symbols to represent the objects. The first problem in the guided-practice section shows how to use the discrete or square-unit model with young learners; this form of the model is also helpful later for multiplication and ratio problems.

When students understand the concept of cardinality, they can move on to the continuous model. At this point, instead of drawing one unit for each object in the problem, they write the appropriate number inside the unit bar. In the blocks-and-dolls example, a student using the continuous model would draw a unit bar. Next he would write "2" inside the unit bar and label it "B" for blocks. He would then write a "4" inside the unit bar and label it "D," drawing vertical lines to divide the unit bar appropriately. Students at this level understand that the "2" represents two blocks and the "4" represents four dolls. They no longer need to draw individual squares in order to understand this concept. Most of the problems in the guided-practice section of this book, and most of the solutions given for the independent-practice section, use the continuous model.

Let's Begin!

To start your work with model drawing, simply read this book and carefully choose examples that are appropriate for your students. I would encourage you to think of model drawing as a strategy that you can call on to supplement virtually any math text you are currently using.

As you work with this wonderful approach, I hope you will both find your own understanding of math enriched and take joy in the successes of your students. I remember a child announcing to me, "I can picture every word problem I read now!" There is no such thing as an ordinary day in teaching, but we do have extraordinary moments, and that was definitely one of them!

Finally, whether this book serves as your introduction to learning and teaching model drawing or as an additional resource to strengthen and deepen your understanding of the model method and how best to use it with students, I hope you will find it a valuable resource. After all, you know what they say about model drawing: it's a picture of success!

Problems for Guided Practice

Addition
(Whole Numbers—Discrete Model)

Janet picked 3 daisies and 2 sunflowers from her garden. How many total flowers did Janet pick from her garden?

Step One: Read the entire problem.

"Janet picked 3 daisies and 2 sunflowers from her garden. How many total flowers did Janet pick from her garden?"

Step Two: Rewrite the question in sentence form, leaving a space for the answer.

Janet picked a total of ___ flowers from her garden.

Step Three: Determine who and/or what is involved in the problem.

*Janet's
flowers*

Step Four: Draw the unit bar(s).

*Janet's
flowers* ☐

Guided Conversation

Step One: Let's read the entire problem and picture what it's about. The problem says that Janet picked 3 daisies and 2 sunflowers. Can you picture both daisies and sunflowers? What word is used to describe these in the question? That's correct. "Flowers" is the common term for daisies and sunflowers.

Step Two: Now look at the question. Who can rewrite this question as a sentence and leave a space for the correct answer? Great: "Janet picked a total of ___ flowers from her garden." When we finish this problem, we'll come back and add the correct total to our sentence.

Step Three: Who and what are involved in this problem? We're talking about Janet in this problem, but Janet's what? Are we talking about her money? Her books? That's right: we're talking about Janet and her flowers. Let's write "Janet's flowers." Remember to use an apostrophe to show that the flowers belong to Janet.

Step Four: We're still setting up the model for our problem, and the next step is to add the unit bar. For this problem, let's begin by drawing one square unit bar. Where should we draw this square? Sure: we'll draw it to the right of "Janet's flowers."

Step Five: Chunk the problem, adjust the unit bars, and fill in the question mark.

A

"Janet picked 3 daisies . . ."

D

Janet's flowers

B

D D D

Janet's flowers

C

". . . and 2 sunflowers from her garden."

D D D S S

Janet's flowers

Step Five—A: Our model is set up! Now let's go back and reread the problem and add the information to our model. Who can read the first sentence? What do we learn? That's correct: we learn that Janet picked 3 daisies and 2 sunflowers from her garden. So part of the flowers she picked are daisies and part of the flowers she picked are sunflowers.

Let's begin with a small chunk: "Janet picked 3 daisies." If we look at our model, we have 1 square unit. Can this square stand for 1 daisy? Sure. Let's add a label above the square unit to show that it stands for 1 daisy. Let's write a "D" for daisy over our square unit.

B: Our problem does not say that Janet picked 1 daisy. What does the problem tell us? Yes, it tells us that she picked 3 daisies. What can we do to our model to show that Janet picked 3 daisies? That's right: we can add 2 more square units. Don't forget to write a "D" over each unit. Just to be sure, let's count. We have 1, 2, 3 square units that stand for daisies.

C: Janet also picked sunflowers. Let's go back to our first sentence for the next chunk of information. How many sunflowers did Janet pick? That's correct: she picked 2 sunflowers. Our model right now shows that Janet picked 3 daisies. How many more square units do we need to add? Yes, let's add 2 more square units. How can we tell these 2 units stand for sunflowers? Great: we can add a label, "S," for each sunflower.

D

"How many total flowers did Janet pick from her garden?"

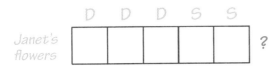

Step Six: Correctly compute and solve the problem.

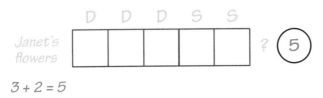

$3 + 2 = 5$

Step Seven: Write the answer in the sentence, and make sure the answer makes sense.

Janet picked a total of _5_ flowers from her garden.

D: Have we included all of the information from the first sentence? Great. Now who can read the last sentence? What kind of sentence is this? That's correct: it's a question. What is the question asking us? Is it asking how many daisies Janet picked? Sunflowers? No, it's asking how many total flowers Janet picked. Where should we put the question mark to show we need to figure out the total or whole amount? Yes, let's write the question mark to the right of our square unit bars. It's usually a good idea to put the total on the right.

Step Six: How are we going to figure out the total number of flowers that Janet picked? I want you each to solve this on your own and then tell me about your answer. I see some of you counted all of the flowers. Someone else wrote a number sentence: "3 + 2 = 5." Great work!

Step Seven: Are we finished? No! We need to go back and add the answer to our sentence. Let's reread our answer and make sure that it makes sense. "Janet picked a total of 5 flowers from her garden." Great work!

Milking the Problem for All It's Worth

■ How many more daisies than sunflowers did Janet pick?

■ If Janet wanted to pick the same number of sunflowers as daisies, how many more sunflowers would she need to pick?

One bag of lettuce weighed 14 ounces. Another bag weighed 12 ounces. What was the total weight of the 2 bags of lettuce?

Guided Conversation

Step One: Read the entire problem.

"One bag of lettuce weighed 14 ounces. Another bag weighed 12 ounces. What was the total weight of the 2 bags of lettuce?"

Step One: Let's read the entire problem to see what is involved.

Step Two: Rewrite the question in sentence form, leaving a space for the answer.

The total weight of the 2 bags of lettuce was ____.

Step Two: Could someone reread the question and help turn it into a sentence? Remember, we'll leave a space for the answer. Great: "The total weight of the 2 bags of lettuce was ____."

Step Three: Determine who and/or what is involved in the problem.

*Weight of
bags of lettuce*

Step Three: Are we talking about a person in this problem? No. What are we talking about? That's correct. We're talking about finding the weight of 2 bags of lettuce. Where and how should we write this? Yes, let's write it on the left side of the paper. Let's write "Weight of bags of lettuce."

Step Four: Draw the unit bar(s).

*Weight of
bags of lettuce*

Step Four: In this next step, we need to draw a unit bar directly to the right of our "who and what." Let's draw a unit bar in the shape of a rectangle.

Step Five: Chunk the problem, adjust the unit bars, and fill in the question mark.

A

"One bag of lettuce weighed 14 ounces."

Weight of bags of lettuce | 1 bag | 14 oz.

B

"Another bag weighed 12 ounces. What was the total weight of the 2 bags of lettuce?"

Weight of bags of lettuce | 1 bag 14 oz. | another bag 12 oz. | ?

Step Five—A: Our model is set up. Are we ready to add the information from the problem? What does the first sentence tell us? That's correct: it says that one bag of lettuce weighed 14 ounces. Does this represent the total weight of the 2 bags or part of the weight? You're right: it stands for part of the weight. This is a part-whole problem. We'll write the parts inside the unit bar. Let's write "14 oz." in the first part of the unit bar, and write a label "1 bag" above it.

B: What does the next sentence tell us? "Another bag weighed 12 ounces"? Is that the total weight or part of the weight of the 2 bags? Great: it's part of the weight. Write "12 oz." inside the unit bar and put the label "another bag" above it. Look at the unit bar. Which part is greater? Correct! We know that 14 ounces is greater than 12 ounces, so let's divide the unit bar with a line that shows this. Finally, what is the question asking us to find? It's asking us to compute the total weight of the 2 bags, so let's write our question mark to the right of the unit bar.

Step Six: Correctly compute and solve the problem.

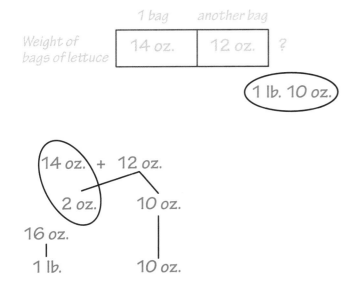

Step Six: It's time to compute. What operation will you use to solve this problem? We've been learning how to think "part-whole" when adding units of measure. Let's practice branching in this example. We're adding ounces to ounces. What's our next unit of measure? Correct! It's a pound. How many ounces are in one pound? Great! There are 16 ounces in one pound. If we write our math expression as "14 oz. + 12 oz.," we can ask, "How many ounces do we need to add to the 14 ounces to make one pound?" Great! We need 2 more ounces. Let's decompose or branch the 12 ounces as 2 ounces and 10 ounces. Now we can see we have 1 pound and 10 ounces. Great work!

Step Seven: Write the answer in the sentence, and make sure the answer makes sense.

The total weight of the 2 bags of lettuce was 26 ounces or 1 pound 10 ounces.

Step Seven: Now let's go back to our sentence and fill in the correct answer. "The total weight of the 2 bags of lettuce was 26 ounces or 1 pound 10 ounces." Is this reasonable? Yes!

Teacher Note

With part-whole problems, students can divide the unit bar to show which numbers are greater than others.

Milking the Problem for All It's Worth

■ How many more ounces of lettuce would be needed to make 2 pounds?

■ What fraction of a pound is the 12-ounce bag?

■ What fraction of a pound is the 14-ounce bag?

Addition
(Whole Numbers with 3 Addends)

A total of 254 people attended a concert on Friday night, 357 attended on Saturday night, and 137 attended on Sunday afternoon. How many total people attended the concert?

Step One: Read the entire problem.

"A total of 254 people attended a concert on Friday night, 357 attended on Saturday night, and 137 attended on Sunday afternoon. How many total people attended the concert?"

Step Two: Rewrite the question in sentence form, leaving a space for the answer.

A total of ___ people attended the concert.

Step Three: Determine who and/or what is involved in the problem.

*People
attending
concert*

Step Four: Draw the unit bar(s).

*People
attending
concert*

Guided Conversation

Step One: Let's read the entire problem and picture what it's about.

Step Two: Who will reread the question and rephrase it as a sentence? Yes: "A total of ___ people attended the concert." Remember, we'll need to come back to our sentence and write in the answer before we finish. Let's focus on our goal of figuring out the total number of people who attended the concert.

Step Three: Who and what are we talking about in this problem? Great! We're talking about people attending the concert. Let's write this on the left side of the paper.

Step Four: Do you remember our next step in setting up our model? Yes, we need to draw a unit bar next to our "who and what."

Step Five: Chunk the problem, adjust the unit bars, and fill in the question mark.

A

"A total of 254 people attended a concert on Friday night, . . ."

People attending concert

Fri.

| 254 |

B

" . . . 357 attended on Saturday night, . . ."

People attending concert

Fri.   Sat.

| 254   357 |

C

" . . . and 137 attended on Sunday afternoon."

People attending concert

Fri.   Sat.   Sun.

| 254   357   137 |

D

"How many total people attended the concert?"

People attending concert

Fri.   Sat.   Sun.

| 254 | 357 | 137 | ?

Step Five—A: Let's reread the first sentence in the problem. There are a lot of numbers in that first sentence. What do you suggest we do? Yes, we'll chunk the information. Let's stop at each comma and add the information to our model. What do we learn first? We discover that 254 people attended a concert on Friday night. Is that all of the people or part of the people attending the concert? It stands for part of the people? Good work! Let's write this part in the unit bar and add "Fri." as a label above it.

B: What do we learn next in the same sentence? We learn that 357 people attended the concert on Saturday night. Again, is this part or all of the people attending the concert? Yes, the number stands for part of the people. Please write "357" in the unit bar and write the label "Sat." above it.

C: Is there more information in the first sentence? Great! We learn that 137 people attended the concert on Sunday afternoon. Again, does this number stand for part or all of the people? That's right: it stands for part of the people. Let's put our last number inside the unit bar and write the label "Sun." above it.

D: In this problem, we can see that we have 3 different numbers of people attending the concert. Please draw lines to divide the values in the unit bar to show which number is greatest and which is least. This gives us an idea of how the values relate to each other.

Finally, what does our question ask us to find? You're correct: we need to find the total attendance. Let's write our question mark to the right of the unit bar.

Step Six: Correctly compute and solve the problem.

	Fri.	Sat.	Sun.	
People attending concert	254	357	137	?

(748)

254 + 357 + 137 = 748

Step Seven: Write the answer in the sentence, and make sure the answer makes sense.

A total of __748__ people attended the concert.

Step Six: What's our next step? Our model is complete, and we have enough information to solve the problem. Please go ahead and solve it on your own. Be ready to explain how you arrived at your answer.

Step Seven: A total of 748 people attended the concert. Let's reflect: is our answer reasonable? Yes, it is!

Milking the Problem for All It's Worth

■ How many people attended the concert on Friday and Saturday nights?

■ How many more people attended the concert on Saturday night than on Friday night?

■ How many more people attended the concert on Saturday night than on Sunday afternoon?

Subtraction
(Whole Numbers—Discrete Model)

There were 6 birds sitting on a tree branch. Two of the birds flew away. How many birds were left?

Step One: Read the entire problem.

"There were 6 birds sitting on a tree branch. Two of the birds flew away. How many birds were left?"

Step Two: Rewrite the question in sentence form, leaving a space for the answer.

There were ___ birds left.

Step Three: Determine who and/or what is involved in the problem.

Birds

Step Four: Draw the unit bar(s).

Birds ☐

Step Five: Chunk the problem, adjust the unit bars, and fill in the question mark.

A
"There were 6 birds sitting on a tree branch."

Birds ☐☐☐☐☐☐ *6*

Guided Conversation

Step One: Let's begin by reading the problem. What are you picturing in your mind? Can you see birds sitting on a branch of a tree, and then can you imagine some of them flying away?

Step Two: Let's look at the question in the problem. How can we write it as a sentence? We need to leave a space for the answer when we write it! Yes, let's write "There were ___ birds left."

Step Three: Can someone tell me who and what we're talking about in this problem? That's right: we're talking about birds. Let's write "Birds" in the space for our model.

Step Four: Let's begin by drawing 1 square unit.

Step Five—A: Now let's go back and read just the first sentence so we can add information in chunks. How many birds does the sentence tell us were sitting on a tree branch? It tells us there were 6? Wonderful! Let's go to our model. Right now we have 1 square unit, which stands for 1 bird. How many square units should be in our model to show there were 6 birds? That's right. Please add more squares until you have a total of 6. Now write a "6" at the end to show the total.

B

"Two of the birds flew away. How many birds were left?"

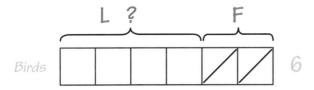

B: What does the next sentence tell us? We learn that 2 birds flew away. Can there still be 6 birds on the branch? No. What do you think we should do to show that 2 birds flew away? Yes, we could erase 2 of the squares. We could also put slashes in 2 of the squares to show that those birds left. Either way is correct. Let's add a brace and write an "F" over those squares to show that those birds flew away.

We have 1 more sentence. What kind of a sentence is it? That's right: it's the question. What does it ask? "How many birds were left?" Let's go to our model and draw a brace over 4 of the square units. Now let's put a question mark there, and let's write an "L" to show that those were birds left. All set!

Step Six: Correctly compute and solve the problem.

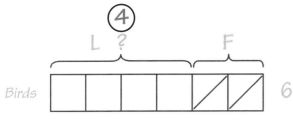

6 − 2 = 4

Step Six: Will each of you now figure out how many birds were left? How did you solve the problem? Some of you counted the number of squares left. I see some of you also wrote a number sentence, "6 − 2 = 4." Well done!

Step Seven: Write the answer in the sentence, and make sure the answer makes sense.

There were _4_ birds left.

Step Seven: Let's add the answer to our sentence and check to be sure it makes sense! "There were 4 birds left." That sounds good to me!

Milking the Problem for All It's Worth

■ If 2 more flew away, how many birds would be left sitting on the tree branch?

■ If still 2 more flew away, how many birds would be left sitting on the tree branch?

Subtraction
(Whole Numbers—Continuous Model)

A total of 438 people were at the concert. There were 213 children and the rest were adults. How many adults were at the concert?

Guided Conversation

Step One: Read the entire problem.

"A total of 438 people were at the concert. There were 213 children and the rest were adults. How many adults were at the concert?"

Step One: Let's begin by reading the problem and picturing what it's about.

Step Two: Rewrite the question in sentence form, leaving a space for the answer.

There were ____ adults at the concert.

Step Two: Next, let's rewrite the question as a sentence and leave a space for the answer. Who can do that for us? Yes: "There were ____ adults at the concert."

Step Three: Determine who and/or what is involved in the problem.

People at concert

Step Three: Who and what are we talking about in this problem? Yes, we're talking about adults and children at a concert. Is there a common term we can use for children and adults? The word is in our first sentence and in the question. Great! Let's use "People at concert."

Step Four: Draw the unit bar(s).

People at concert [ ]

Step Four: What is our next step in setting up the model? Good: we draw a unit bar.

Step Five: Chunk the problem, adjust the unit bars, and fill in the question mark.

A

"A total of 438 people were at the concert."

People at concert [ ] 438

Step Five—A: Are we ready to begin adding information to the model? What does the first sentence tell us? Yes, it tells us that a total of 438 people were at the concert. If 438 is the total, where should we write that number in our model? To the right of the unit bar? Wonderful!

B

"There were 213 children and the rest were adults."

C

"How many adults were at the concert?"

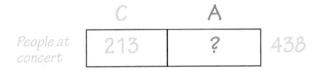

Step Six: Correctly compute and solve the problem.

C   A

People at   213   ?   438
concert

⟨225⟩

438 – 213 = 225

Step Seven: Write the answer in the sentence, and make sure the answer makes sense.

There were 225 adults at the concert.

B: Please reread the next sentence. What do we learn? Sure: of all of the people at the concert, 213 were children. Only part of our total represents children. Where should we write this number? Okay. Let's write it inside the unit bar and write the label "C" above it.

C: Let's finish with the question. "How many adults were at the concert?" Were some or all of the people at the concert adults? You're right: only some were adults, and our question is asking how many. Where should we write the question mark? Good. Let's write our question mark inside the unit bar and write an "A" above it. Please draw a line to separate the 2 parts in the unit bar.

Step Six: Look at your model. Do you notice that we know the total number of people and the total number of children at the concert? Our job is to find how many adults were at the concert. Can you see why we call this a "whole-part" problem? We know the total and one of the parts. Now go ahead and solve this on your own.

I see some of you have written "213 + ___ = 438." Do you remember working with smaller number bonds, such as 2 + ___ = 8? Back then, you could "count on" to figure out the missing number. Now I see most of you subtracting to find the missing number. That's great!

Step Seven: There were 225 adults at the concert. Does that make sense? It sure does!

Milking the Problem for All It's Worth

■ How many more adults than children were at the concert?

■ If 17 more children came, what would be the new total number of people at the concert?

Subtraction
(Whole Numbers—Comparison)

Rico has $45. Tom has $28. How much more money does Rico have than Tom?

Step One: Read the entire problem.

"Rico has $45. Tom has $28. How much more money does Rico have than Tom?"

Step Two: Rewrite the question in sentence form, leaving a space for the answer.

Rico has $____ more than Tom.

Step Three: Determine who and/or what is involved in the problem.

Rico's money

Tom's money

Step Four: Draw the unit bar(s).

Rico's money [   ]

Tom's money [   ]

Guided Conversation

Step One: Let's begin by reading the problem and picturing what it's about.

Step Two: Our next step is to rewrite the question as a sentence. We'll leave a space for the answer, which we can fill in later. What could we say? Sure: "Rico has $____ more than Tom."

Step Three: Who and what are we talking about in this problem? That's correct: we're talking about Rico's money and Tom's money. We want to list both names in our model. Let's do that on the left side of the paper. Be sure to write their names in the order they appear in the problem.

Step Four: When we have 2 variables, we give each one a separate unit bar. We need to draw unit bars of equal size and value next to "Rico's money" and "Tom's money." Now this is important. Right now does the model—before we add information from the problem—make it look like Rico and Tom have the same amount of money? You're right: it does look that way. It's time to reread our problem and adjust our unit bars to make them correct.

Step Five: Chunk the problem, adjust the unit bars, and fill in the question mark.

A

"Rico has $45."

| Rico's money | | $45 |

| Tom's money | |

B

"Tom has $28."

| Rico's money | | $45 |

| Tom's money | $28 | |

C

"How much more money does Rico have than Tom?"

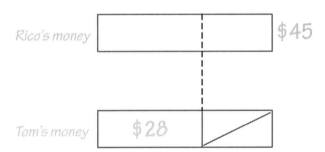

Step Five—A: What does our first sentence tell us? Yes, Rico has $45. Let's go to the unit bar next to "Rico's money" and write "$45" to the right of it. That's Rico's total.

B: Who can read the next sentence? Yes, "Tom has $28." Let's go to Tom's unit bar. Right now Tom's unit bar is the same size and has the same value as Rico's, doesn't it? But does Tom have the same amount of money as Rico? No, he has less money. He has only $28. In other words, can you see that Tom has only part of what Rico has? Let's write "$28" inside of Tom's unit bar. We can draw a slash through the last part of Tom's unit bar to show he has only part of $45.

C: It's time to read the last sentence, which is the question. "How much more money does Rico have than Tom?" Let's compare the 2 unit bars. Which parts are still the same? Do you notice how we can draw a dotted vertical line to show the parts of Rico's and Tom's unit bars that are the same? The first part of each unit bar has what value? $28? Great!

D

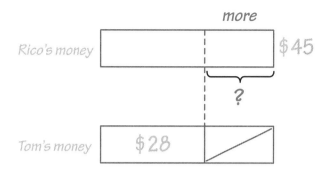

D: Now we need to place the question mark. Look at the unit bars. Can you see the parts that are the same? Where in Rico's unit bar does it show that he has more? Correct: the second part of his unit bar shows how much more Rico has than Tom. Our goal is to figure out how much more. Notice how we draw a brace under this part and write in our question mark. Let's write "more" over that part of Rico's unit bar. Now can you see why we drew the slash in the second part of Tom's unit bar? It shows he does not have that part. Good job comparing and learning!

Step Six: Correctly compute and solve the problem.

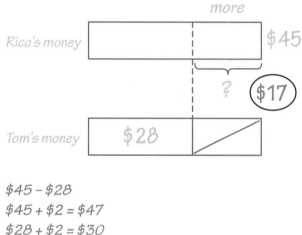

$45 – $28
$45 + $2 = $47
$28 + $2 = $30
$47 – $30 = $17

Step Six: Now that our model is finished, how will you solve the problem? I see that most of you are subtracting to find the difference between $28 and $45. It's great that one of you used compensation to do the subtraction. I see that you wrote this:

$45 – $28
$45 + $2 = $47
$28 + $2 = $30
$47 – $30 = $17

Step Seven: Write the answer in the sentence, and make sure the answer makes sense.

Rico has $17 more than Tom.

Step Seven: Are we finished? No, we need to add the answer to our sentence and check to be sure it's reasonable. "Rico has $17 more than Tom." Does our answer make sense? Yes!

Teacher Note

When doing a subtraction comparison problem, some students learn best by actually adjusting one of the unit bars—erasing and making that bar shorter to show that it represents the lesser amount. Building understanding is the goal. Do what will make the most sense to the student.

Milking the Problem for All It's Worth

■ How much money do Rico and Tom have altogether?

■ How much more money would Tom need to have a total of $50?

Multiplication
(Whole Numbers—Single-Digit Factor)

Ling put 3 photos on each page of her album. If there were 6 pages, how many photos did Ling put in her album?

Step One: Read the entire problem.

"Ling put 3 photos on each page of her album. If there were 6 pages, how many photos did Ling put in her album?"

Step Two: Rewrite the question in sentence form, leaving a space for the answer.

Ling put a total of ____ photos in her album.

Step Three: Determine who and/or what is involved in the problem.

*Ling's
photos*

Step Four: Draw the unit bar(s).

*Ling's
photos*

Guided Conversation

Step One: Let's begin by reading the problem. Can you picture 6 pages of a photo album, and someone putting 3 photos on each page?

Step Two: The next step is to rewrite the question as a sentence, leaving a space for the answer that we'll add later. Who can do this? Good. "Ling put a total of ___ photos in her album." This helps us picture the problem we need to solve.

Step Three: Who and what are we talking about in this problem? Great! We're talking about Ling's photos. Rewriting the question as a sentence helps us with this step, doesn't it?

Step Four: What do we need to add to our model now? Yes, a unit bar. In Step One, when we read the problem and pictured what it was about, we talked about visualizing 6 pages with 3 photos on each page. For this type of problem, let's use the square unit to begin, because we are going to draw 6 equal units to model the number of pages. Can you see that if we draw 6 long units, we might not even have room on the page? The goal in multiplication is to actually see that we have equal groups of some number. So let's use the square units for multiplication.

Step Five: Chunk the problem, adjust the unit bars, and fill in the question mark.

A

"Ling put 3 photos on each page of her album."

B

"If there were 6 pages, . . ."

Ling's photos	pg.	pg.	pg.	pg.	pg.	pg.
	3	3	3	3	3	3

C

". . . how many photos did Ling put in her album?"

Ling's photos	pg.	pg.	pg.	pg.	pg.	pg.	
	3	3	3	3	3	3	?

Step Six: Correctly compute and solve the problem.

Ling's photos	pg.	pg.	pg.	pg.	pg.	pg.	
	3	3	3	3	3	3	?

⑱

$6 \times 3 = 18$

Step Five—A: It's time to reread the problem and add the information to our model in chunks. Ready? What does the first sentence tell us? Sure: "Ling put 3 photos on each page of her album." Let's go to the model. We have 1 small (square) unit bar right now, don't we? If we write the label "pg." for page over this unit, and put "3" inside the bar, we have one page with 3 photos represented in our model.

B: Let's move on to the next sentence. "If there were 6 pages." Do you see the comma? Let's stop and add this information to the model. What does our model show right now? Very good! It shows 1 page with 3 photos on it. How many more equal units do we need to add to show a total of 6 pages? Great! Please add 5 more. Write the label "pg." over each unit and a "3" inside each one. Let's stop and read our model. Do you see the 6 pages of the album, with 3 photos on each page? Good!

C: It's time to go back and finish the last sentence. What is the question? Excellent! We need to figure out the total number of photos Ling put in her album. Where should the question mark go if we want to find the total? Sure: to the right of the unit bar.

Step Six: Our model is ready. Are you? Please look at the wonderful model of this problem. Do you see 6 equal groups of 3? Can you see why multiplication is really repeated addition? The model-drawing strategy helps us understand the problem and visualize the operation we need to use to solve it.

I see a few solutions. Some of you did repeated addition. I also see "6 × 3 = 18." Nice work!

Step Seven: Write the answer in the sentence, and make sure the answer makes sense.

Ling put a total of 18 photos in her album.

Step Seven: Are we finished? No. We need to add the answer to our sentence and be sure it makes sense, don't we? "Ling put a total of 18 photos in her album." Does that make sense? Absolutely!

Milking the Problem for All It's Worth

- How many photos could Ling put in her album if there were 9 pages?

- How many photos could Ling put in her album if she could put 4 photos on each of the 6 pages?

Teacher Note

If your students are familiar with division, take the time to share how the model shows that division is the inverse of multiplication. We can see that 6 groups of 3 make 18, and we can also see that 18 divided into 6 equal groups makes 3 in each group.

Luis ran 2 miles each day during the month of September. How many total miles did Luis run in September?

Step One: Read the entire problem.

"Luis ran 2 miles each day during the month of September. How many total miles did Luis run in September?"

Step Two: Rewrite the question in sentence form, leaving a space for the answer.

Luis ran a total of ___ miles in September.

Step Three: Determine who and/or what is involved in the problem.

Luis's mi.

Step Four: Draw the unit bar(s).

Luis's mi.

Step Five: Chunk the problem, adjust the unit bars, and fill in the question mark.

A

"Luis ran 2 miles each day during the month of September."

Luis's mi.   Sept.1
2

Step One: Let's begin by reading the problem. Can you picture what it's about as we read?

Step Two: Let's rewrite the question as a sentence and leave a space for the answer. This helps us visualize the problem we are solving. Good: "Luis ran a total of ___ miles in September."

Step Three: Who and what are we talking about in this problem? Yes, we're talking about Luis's miles. Please write that to begin your model.

Step Four: What's the next step? Draw a unit bar next to the variable? Sure!

Step Five—A: It's time to begin illustrating the problem in our model. Look at the first sentence. "Luis ran 2 miles each day during the month of September." Let's mark off a unit at the beginning of our bar and write "2" inside. Then, above it, add the label "Sept. 1."

B

Sept. 1   Sept. 30

Luis's mi. | 2 | | 2 |

B: But the problem does not say that Luis ran 2 miles only on September first. It says he ran 2 miles each day of September. What do we need to know to continue modeling? Great! We need to know the number of days in September. Who knows that number? 30? You bet! How can we show this on our unit bar? We could draw 30 units and write "2" in each one, but would that be a good use of our time and paper? Let me show you how we can model multiplication when large numbers are involved. Look back at the unit bar. We've already labeled the first unit "Sept. 1" and we wrote "2" inside the unit. Now let's go to the end of our unit bar and create a final unit that we can label "Sept. 30." Also, write a "2" inside that unit.

C

"How many total miles did Luis run in September?"

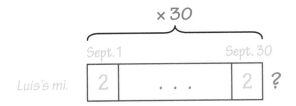

C: Now, in between the first and final units, we can put an ellipsis. An ellipsis is three dots that indicate the pattern continues between the first and final values. It is a symbol that saves us from having to draw 30 equal units. Let's also add a brace above the whole thing and write " × 30" to show that there are 30 units in all. All set? Great!

Are we finished? No. We have one more sentence, which is our question. "How many total miles did Luis run in September?" Where should we put the question mark in our model? To the right of the unit bar? Sure, because we're finding the total miles Luis ran.

Step Six: Correctly compute and solve the problem.

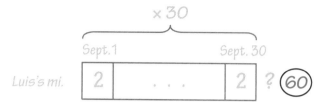

$30 \times 2 \text{ mi.} = 60 \text{ mi.}$

Step Seven: Write the answer in the sentence, and make sure the answer makes sense.

Luis ran a total of 60 miles in September.

Step Six: It's time for you to work your computation off to the side or underneath the problem. I see that many of you wrote "30 × 2 mi. = 60 mi." Did anyone solve it differently?

Step Seven: Are we finished? No! Let's add the answer to our statement and make sure it's reasonable. "Luis ran a total of 60 miles in September." Does that make sense? It does! Good work!

Milking the Problem for All It's Worth

■ If Luis runs the same number of miles each day in October, how many more miles will he run in October than in September?

■ What if Luis runs only a mile each day? How many total miles will he run in September?

Teacher Note

Modeling this type of problem helps solidify a student's visualization and understanding of multiplying a small number by a large number. (I usually suggest this approach when multiplying by a factor greater than 10.)

Multiplication
(Comparison)

9

Itty and Bitty each did jumping jacks. Itty did 8 jumping jacks. Bitty did 4 times as many jumping jacks as Itty. How many jumping jacks did Itty and Bitty do altogether?

Guided Conversation

Step One: Read the entire problem.

"Itty and Bitty each did jumping jacks. Itty did 8 jumping jacks. Bitty did 4 times as many jumping jacks as Itty. How many jumping jacks did Itty and Bitty do altogether?"

Step One: Let's begin by reading the problem and picturing what it's about.

Step Two: Rewrite the question in sentence form, leaving a space for the answer.

Itty and Bitty did ___ jumping jacks altogether.

Step Two: Who can rewrite the question as a sentence, leaving a space for the answer? Good: "Itty and Bitty did ___ jumping jacks altogether."

Step Three: Determine who and/or what is involved in the problem.

*Itty's
jumping jacks*

*Bitty's
jumping jacks*

Step Three: How many people are involved in this problem? Sure. There are 2 people: Itty and Bitty. We're talking about their what? Good: their jumping jacks! Let's begin our model by writing "Itty's jumping jacks" and "Bitty's jumping jacks." Be sure to leave space between these 2 variables.

Step Four: Draw the unit bar(s).

*Itty's
jumping jacks*

*Bitty's
jumping jacks*

Step Four: What is our next step? We need to add the unit bars? That's right! Let's go to "Itty's jumping jacks" and draw a square unit. Next, let's go to "Bitty's jumping jacks" and also draw a square unit that's the same size and value as Itty's. Right now, in our model, does it look like Itty and Bitty did the same number of jumping jacks? It certainly does. It's time to make it correct by rereading the problem and adding new information to our model.

Step Five: Chunk the problem, adjust the unit bars, and fill in the question mark.

A

"Itty and Bitty each did jumping jacks. Itty did 8 jumping jacks."

Itty's
jumping jacks   [8]

Bitty's
jumping jacks   [   ]

B

"Bitty did 4 times as many jumping jacks as Itty."

Itty's
jumping jacks   [8]

Bitty's
jumping jacks   [| | |]

Step Five—A: Please read the first sentence. "Itty and Bitty each did jumping jacks." Let's look at our model. Is there anything new to add? No. We already have this information written. Let's move on to the next sentence. "Itty did 8 jumping jacks." Again, stop and go to the model. What should we add? Sure. Let's write an "8" inside Itty's unit. All set?

B: What about the next sentence? "Bitty did 4 times as many jumping jacks as Itty." Please look at the model. Right now it looks like Itty and Bitty did the same number of jumping jacks, doesn't it? But what information did we just learn? Yes, we learned that Bitty did 4 times as many as Itty. Let's make our model correct! If we add one more unit to Bitty's model, what does it show? Yes, it shows that Bitty did 2 times or twice as many jumping jacks as Itty. Is this what the problem says? No! Let's add another equal unit to Bitty's model. What does our model say now? It says that Bitty did 3 times as many jumping jacks as Itty? Good! Is it correct? No! Okay. Add one more equal unit to Bitty's model. How many total square units does Bitty have in her model now? Is our model correct now? Does it match the facts in the problem? Great! It does. It shows that Bitty did 4 times as many jumping jacks as Itty.

Teacher Note

When using model drawing to solve problems that involve multiplication and comparisons (such as 4 times as many), I encourage students to use the discrete or square units. This allows sufficient space to model the problem, and it also reinforces the concept that multiplication involves equal groups of some number.

C

"How many jumping jacks did Itty and Bitty do altogether?"

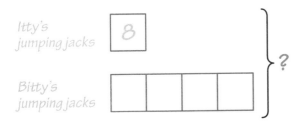

Step Six: Correctly compute and solve the problem.

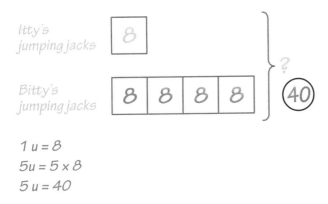

$1 u = 8$
$5u = 5 \times 8$
$5 u = 40$

Step Seven: Write the answer in the sentence, and make sure the answer makes sense.

Itty and Bitty did 40 jumping jacks altogether.

C: Let's finish by rereading the final sentence, which is the question. "How many jumping jacks did Itty and Bitty do altogether?" Watch as I show you how to write the question mark in a problem when we are finding the total for more than one variable. We'll still go to the right of both unit bars, but we'll draw a brace next to them. Now write the question mark to the right of the brace. Good work!

Step Six: Now that we've finished translating the problem into our model, it's time to compute and find the total. Do we have a problem in our model? I see 4 equal units next to Bitty, but I don't see any values in those units. Can you talk with your partner or think to yourself about the value of each of Bitty's units? Great explanation! Each of Bitty's units is the same size and has the same value as Itty's unit. Since Itty's unit has a value of 8, each of Bitty's must also have a value of 8. Now do you have enough information to compute the answer? I see different people solved it in different ways, but you all arrived at a total of 40 jumping jacks for both girls.

Step Seven: Let's add the answer to our sentence. "Itty and Bitty did 40 jumping jacks altogether." Is the answer reasonable? Yes!

Milking the Problem for All It's Worth

- How many more jumping jacks did Bitty do than Itty?
- What fraction of the total number of jumping jacks did Bitty do?
- What fraction of the total number of jumping jacks did Itty do?

Simon arranged chairs in the gym for an assembly. He put 42 chairs into 6 equal rows. How many chairs were in each row?

Step One: Read the entire problem.

"Simon arranged chairs in the gym for an assembly. He put 42 chairs into 6 equal rows. How many chairs were in each row?"

Step One: Let's read the problem and picture what it's about.

Step Two: Rewrite the question in sentence form, leaving a space for the answer.

There were ____ chairs in each row.

Step Two: Next, let's rewrite the question as a sentence and leave a space for the answer. Can someone do that? "There were ____ chairs in each row." Excellent!

Step Three: Determine who and/or what is involved in the problem.

*Chairs
in rows*

Step Three: Now we need to identify the "who and what" or the variable in this problem. Simon's chairs in rows? Sure. I want you to think about this. Does Simon need to be listed or simply "Chairs in rows"? Good. We can write "Chairs in rows." In this particular problem, we don't need to know the name of the person. It would certainly be okay if we wrote Simon's name, but we don't need to in this case.

Step Four: Draw the unit bar(s).

*Chairs
in rows* [ ]

Step Four: The next step is to draw the unit bar next to the variable.

Step Five: Chunk the problem, adjust the unit bars, and fill in the question mark.

A

"Simon arranged chairs in the gym for an assembly. He put 42 chairs . . ."

Chairs in rows [   ] 42

B

". . . into 6 equal rows. How many chairs were in each row?"

Chairs in rows | R | R | R | R | R | R |
| ? | | | | | | 42

Step Six: Correctly compute and solve the problem.

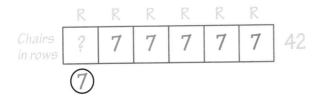

6 u = 42
1 u = 42 ÷ 6
1 u = 7

Step Five—A: The model is set up, so let's reread the problem, one sentence at a time. Please read the first sentence. Do we learn anything that needs to be added to our model? No. Let's continue with the next sentence. "He put 42 chairs into 6 equal rows." Remember, we're going to chunk the information, so let's pause after "42 chairs" and add this to our model. Where should we write the "42"? To the right of the unit bar, because 42 represents the total number of chairs? Great!

B: What should we do next? Yes, let's return to finish the sentence: "into 6 equal rows." What should we do to show this with our unit bar? Divide the unit bar into 6 equal units and write the label "R" for row above each unit? Good. We can now read our model and see that there are 42 chairs divided into 6 equal rows. It's time to read the question: "How many chairs were in each row?" Where should we write the question mark? Good! We can write it in any one of the units, because with division, once we find the value of one unit, we know the value for each unit. I usually put the question mark in the first unit.

Step Six: Please solve the problem on your own. I see a paper with "42 ÷ 6 = 7." Can we add 7 to each of our units, so we can see that the value of each unit is 7? Do you also see how division and multiplication are related?

Step Seven: Write the answer in the sentence, and make sure the answer makes sense.

There were 7 chairs in each row.

Step Seven: Please add your answer to the sentence. "There were 7 chairs in each row." Make sure it makes sense!

Teacher Note

This problem is an example of a partitive division problem. With this type of division, we know the total and the number of groups. Our goal is to find the number in *each* group.

Milking the Problem for All It's Worth

- How many chairs would Simon put in each row if he wanted 7 equal rows?

- How many chairs would be left over if Simon put the 42 chairs into 8 equal rows?

Division
(Whole Numbers with Remainder—Quotitive or Measurement)

Mr. Rodriguez is finding drivers to take 17 of his students on a field trip. If only 4 students can ride in each car, how many cars will Mr. Rodriguez need?

Step One: Read the entire problem.

"Mr. Rodriguez is finding drivers to take 17 of his students on a field trip. If only 4 students can ride in each car, how many cars will Mr. Rodriguez need?"

Step Two: Rewrite the question in sentence form, leaving a space for the answer.

Mr. Rodriguez will need ___ cars for the field trip.

Step Three: Determine who and/or what is involved in the problem.

Students in cars

Step Four: Draw the unit bar(s).

Students in cars [ ]

Step Five: Chunk the problem, adjust the unit bars, and fill in the question mark.

A
"Mr. Rodriguez is finding drivers to take 17 of his students on a field trip."

Students in cars [ ] 17

Guided Conversation

Step One: Let's read the problem and picture what it's about.

Step Two: The next step is to rewrite the question as a sentence, leaving a space for the answer. Can someone suggest a good sentence? "Mr. Rodriguez will need ___ cars for the field trip"? Sure!

Step Three: Who and what are involved in this problem? Good. We're talking about students in cars.

Step Four: What should we do next to set up our model? Draw a unit bar? Good!

Step Five—A: Let's go back and reread the problem and add the information to our model in chunks. What does the first sentence tell us? Yes: "Mr. Rodriguez is finding drivers to take 17 of his students on a field trip." Where should we write "17" in our model? Very good. The "17" represents the total number of students who need rides. Let's write "17" to the right of the unit bar.

B

"If only 4 students can ride in each car, . . ."

C

". . . how many cars will Mr. Rodriguez need?"

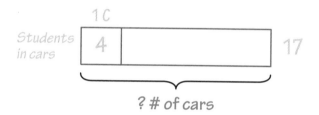

B: Okay, let's continue with the next sentence. "If only 4 students can ride in each car." Let's pause and add this chunk of information to our model. Please notice that the problem does not say there are 4 cars and ask how many students can ride in each car. The problem tells us that only 4 students can ride in each car, and it asks how many cars Mr. Rodriguez will need. Let me show you how to model this. Let's go to the far left of our unit bar and create one unit, writing "4" inside and writing the label "1 C" (for "car") above it. Our model now shows what we know so far.

C: Let's continue by finishing the question part of the final sentence: "how many cars will Mr. Rodriguez need?" Where do you think the question mark should go? Talk it over with a partner or think about it to yourself. The problem is not asking how many students are in each car, so we won't put the question mark inside a unit. Watch. We'll draw a brace under the entire unit bar and write the question mark like this: "? # of cars."

Step Six: Correctly compute and solve the problem.

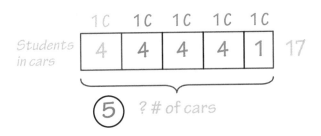

17
– 4   – 1 car (1)
13
– 4   – 1 car (2)
9
– 4   – 1 car (3)
5
– 4   – 1 car (4)
1   – 1 car (5)

Step Seven: Write the answer in the sentence, and make sure the answer makes sense.

Mr. Rodriguez will need 5 cars for the field trip.

Step Six: Again, talk with your partner or think on your own about how to solve this problem. If each unit represents 1 car with 4 students, then it really helps to look at the model to try to visualize the number of groups of 4 you can make from 17. Each group stands for a car that will be needed. I see different solutions around the class. I notice one answer is "4 R1." What is wrong with this answer? Can you have a remainder 1 car? This kind of answer is what you get when you just do the math procedure without checking to see if that answer is reasonable. Another solution I see looks like this: "17 – 4 = 13; 13 – 4 = 9; 9 – 4 = 5; 5 – 4 = 1." The student used repeated subtraction to find there are 4 groups of 4, with 1 student left over. But I see this student wrote "5 cars," because we still need a car for that last student. Good thinking! Some division problems ask us not how many are in each group, but instead, how many groups—or in this example, how many cars.

Step Seven: Don't forget to make sure your answer makes sense, and then add it to your sentence. "Mr. Rodriguez will need 5 cars for the field trip."

Milking the Problem for All It's Worth

■ If 2 more students decide to go on the field trip, how many cars will be needed?

■ If 3 fewer students decide to go on the field trip, how many cars will be needed?

12 Mixed Operations
(Whole Numbers—Addition & Subtraction)

Jerome's goal is to read 345 pages of his book over a 3-day period. If he reads 142 pages on Monday and 115 pages on Tuesday, how many pages will Jerome need to read on Wednesday to reach his goal?

Step One: Read the entire problem.

"Jerome's goal is to read 345 pages of his book over a 3-day period. If he reads 142 pages on Monday and 115 pages on Tuesday, how many pages will Jerome need to read on Wednesday to reach his goal?"

Step One: Let's read the problem to get a picture of what it's all about.

Step Two: Rewrite the question in sentence form, leaving a space for the answer.

Jerome will need to read ___ pages on Wednesday to reach his goal.

Step Two: Look at the question. Who can rewrite this question as a sentence, leaving a space for the answer that we'll add later? Good: "Jerome will need to read ___ pages on Wednesday to reach his goal."

Step Three: Determine who and/or what is involved in the problem.

Jerome's pages

Step Three: Who and what are we talking about in this problem? Jerome's pages? Very good. Let's begin the model by writing this.

Step Four: Draw the unit bar(s).

Jerome's pages ▭

Step Four: What is our next step? Sure: we need to draw a unit bar in the model.

Step Five: Chunk the problem, adjust the unit bars, and fill in the question mark.

A

"Jerome's goal is to read 345 pages of his book . . ."

Jerome's pages [   ] 345

B

". . . over a 3-day period. If he reads 142 pages on Monday . . ."

Jerome's pages | M [142   ] 345

C

". . . and 115 pages on Tuesday, . . ."

Jerome's pages | M | T [142 | 115] 345

Step Five—A: Are you ready to reread the problem and finish building our model? What does the first sentence tell us? "Jerome's goal is to read 345 pages of his book over a 3-day period." Let's add this information in chunks. Let's begin with the 345 pages. What does this number represent? It's the total number of pages Jerome wants to read? Good. Where should we write the total? To the right of the unit bar? Sure.

B: Let's move on to the next chunk of information in this sentence: "over a 3-day period." Into how many parts will we be dividing this unit bar? Yes, we'll divide it into 3 parts. Will each part be equal? No, the parts will not be equal. Jerome does not read the same number of pages each day. Let's divide the bar as we add information. When we're finished, though, our unit bar should have 3 different parts—one for Monday, one for Tuesday, and one for Wednesday.

Okay, let's move ahead to the next sentence, which begins, "If he reads 142 pages on Monday." Let's pause and add this chunk of information to the model. This number stands for part of the pages Jerome reads, so put it inside the unit bar and write the label "M" above it.

C: Let's continue: "and 115 pages on Tuesday." Another part? Yes. Put that number in the unit bar and write the label "T" above it. Which number is greater, 142 or 115? Divide these 2 parts. Can you believe that we're still working on the same sentence?

D

". . . how many pages will Jerome need to read on Wednesday to reach his goal?"

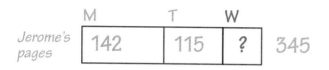

Step Six: Correctly compute and solve the problem.

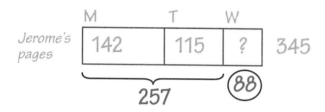

A. 142 + 115 = 257

B. 345 − 257 = 88

D: Let's go back and finish the question portion of the last sentence! It asks, "how many pages will Jerome need to read on Wednesday to reach his goal?" Where should we write the question mark for this model? Great! Put it in the last part of the unit bar and write the label "W" above it. Now let's draw a line to separate Tuesday from Wednesday in the unit bar.

Step Six: It's time to solve this problem. What do we know? We know the total and 2 of the parts. How can we find the third part? Is this a 1-step problem? No, it's a 2-step problem! What should we do first? Great! Let's first add together the pages Jerome is reading on Monday and Tuesday. What's the total? Good work! The total is 257. How will we now figure out how many pages Jerome needs to read on Wednesday? We just need to subtract 257 from 345. Do you remember back to the days when you could figure this out with small numbers just by counting on? Now, it's much more efficient to subtract!

What is your answer? Jerome will need to read 88 pages on Wednesday? Good. Let's add the answer and circle it in the model. Do you need to do some adjusting? Please divide your unit bar to show unequal amounts. Which part is the longest? Which part is the shortest? Good thinking!

Step Seven: Write the answer in the sentence, and make sure the answer makes sense.

Jerome will need to read 88 pages on Wednesday to reach his goal.

Step Seven: Are we finished? No. We need to add the answer to our sentence and check to make sure it makes sense. "Jerome will need to read 88 pages on Wednesday to reach his goal." Does it make sense? Absolutely!

Milking the Problem for All It's Worth

■ How many more pages did Jerome read on Monday than on Tuesday?

■ If Jerome decided to read 382 pages instead of 345, how many more pages would he need to read on Wednesday to reach his goal?

Sasha picked 6 baskets of apples, putting 10 apples in each basket. She then divided the baskets of apples evenly among 3 people. How many apples did Sasha give each of the 3 people?

Step One: Read the entire problem.

"Sasha picked 6 baskets of apples, putting 10 apples in each basket. She then divided the baskets of apples evenly among 3 people. How many apples did Sasha give each of the 3 people?"

Step One: Let's begin by reading the problem. Is Sasha just putting apples in baskets? No, Sasha's first putting apples into baskets; then, she's dividing the baskets of apples evenly among 3 people.

Step Two: Rewrite the question in sentence form, leaving a space for the answer.

Sasha gave each person ___ apples.

Step Two: Let's rewrite the question as a sentence and leave a space for the answer we will add when we finish the problem. Can someone do that? Sure: "Sasha gave each person ___ apples."

Step Three: Determine who and/or what is involved in the problem.

*Sasha's
apples*

Step Three: Now who and what are we talking about in this problem? Good! We're talking about Sasha's apples. Let's write that in our model.

Step Four: Draw the unit bar(s).

*Sasha's
apples*

Step Four: Next, what should we do? Yes, draw a unit bar.

Step Five: Chunk the problem, adjust the unit bars, and fill in the question mark.

A

"Sasha picked 6 baskets of apples, putting 10 apples in each basket."

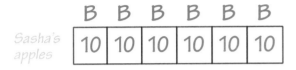

B

"She then divided the baskets of apples evenly among 3 people. How many apples did Sasha give each of the 3 people?"

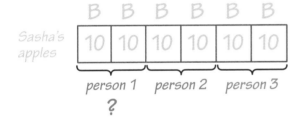

Step Five—A: Now that our model is set up, let's begin by rereading the problem. What does the first sentence tell us? Sure! "Sasha picked 6 baskets of apples, putting 10 apples in each basket." Let's chunk the information. "Sasha picked 6 baskets of apples" is our first chunk. Where and how should we show this in our model? Great! Go to the unit bar and divide it into 6 equal units. Then write the label "B" over each one. We can now see Sasha's 6 baskets.

Let's finish the sentence: "putting 10 apples in each basket." Well, how easy is this? Write "10" in each of the 6 units. We're finished with our first sentence. The model matches the words in the problem.

B: Let's continue with the second sentence. "She then divided the baskets of apples evenly among 3 people." Look at the model. How can we show that we are dividing the 6 baskets or units among 3 people? Good. We can divide the 6 units into groups of 2. Let's put a brace under each group of 2. We can label the braces "person 1," "person 2," and "person 3." Let's finish reading the problem. What does the question ask? "How many apples did Sasha give each of the 3 people?" That's right. Where should we put the question mark? Sure: under one of the groups, because the question asks how many apples Sasha gave *each* person.

Step Six: Correctly compute and solve the problem.

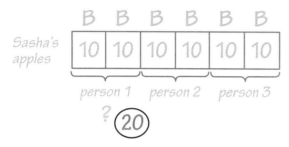

Sasha's apples

B B B B B B
10 10 10 10 10 10

person 1   person 2   person 3

? (20)

1 u = 10
2 u = 2 × 10
2 u = 20

Step Seven: Write the answer in the sentence, and make sure the answer makes sense.

Sasha gave each person 20 apples.

Step Six: Please work with your group or on your own to solve this problem. Who can explain how they got their answer? Great! One group divided the 6 units into 3 groups, showing 2 units in each group. Then I see you multiplied 2 × 10 to find that 1 person received 20 apples. I also see that another group figured out the total number of apples that Sasha put into all of the baskets, which was 60. Then you divided the total number of apples by 3 to get an answer of 20. Excellent work!

Step Seven: Let's add the answer to our sentence: "Sasha gave each person 20 apples." Is our answer reasonable? Sure!

Milking the Problem for All It's Worth

■ How many apples would each person get if Sasha divided them evenly between 2 people?

■ How would the answer change if Sasha put 12 apples in each basket?

Fractions
(Addition)

Marissa spent $\frac{2}{3}$ of her money at the mall and had $10 left. How much money did she spend at the mall?

Step One: Read the entire problem.

"Marissa spent $\frac{2}{3}$ of her money at the mall and had $10 left. How much money did she spend at the mall?"

Step Two: Rewrite the question in sentence form, leaving a space for the answer.

Marissa spent $ ___ at the mall.

Step Three: Determine who and/or what is involved in the problem.

*Marissa's
money*

Step Four: Draw the unit bar(s).

*Marissa's
money* [ ]

Guided Conversation

Step One: Let's begin by reading the problem and picturing what it's about.

Step Two: Who can rewrite our question as a sentence, leaving a space for the answer? Wonderful! "Marissa spent $ ___ at the mall."

Step Three: Who and what are involved in this problem? Correct: we're talking about Marissa's money.

Step Four: What should we do next to set up our model? Draw a unit bar next to "Marissa's money"? Great! When a word problem includes a fraction, that is a clue to draw a long unit bar in our model. Let's do that now.

Step Five: Chunk the problem, adjust the unit bars, and fill in the question mark.

A

"Marissa spent $\frac{2}{3}$ of her money at the mall . . ."

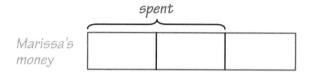

B

" . . . and had $10 left. How much money did she spend at the mall?"

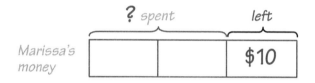

Step Five—A: Are you ready for the next step? Let's go back and reread the problem and chunk the information. The first sentence tells us that Marissa spent $\frac{2}{3}$ of her money and had $10 left. That's too much information! What's our first chunk? That's right: the problem tells us that Marissa spent $\frac{2}{3}$ of her money. Did she spend all or part of her money? She spent part or $\frac{2}{3}$ of it? Good. How can we show this with our unit bar? Absolutely. Divide the unit bar into 3 equal parts, and then draw a brace above 2 of the parts. Let's add the label "spent" above the brace.

B: Are we finished with the first sentence? No, we still need to add that Marissa had $10 left. How should we show this? That's right: the final unit or final $\frac{1}{3}$ stands for the money she had left, so we can write "$10" in this $\frac{1}{3}$ and add the label "left" above it. Let's put a brace there, too. Great!

Now what should we do? That's right: model the final sentence, which is the question. "How much money did she spend at the mall?" Where should we write the question mark? We won't put it to the right of the unit bar, because that would mean we were trying to find the total amount of money Marissa took to the mall. What part of our model answers the question? That's right! Write the question mark next to the label "spent." That's what we are asked to find.

Step Six: Correctly compute and solve the problem.

$10 + $10 = $20

Step Six: It's time to compute, but I don't see values in each of the 3 units. The final unit has a value of $10. How can this help us? We can work backward? Great thinking. We know that the units are equal, so they must each have the same value. If the final $\frac{1}{3}$ has a value of $10, then each $\frac{1}{3}$ must have a value of $10. Let's add these numbers to our model. Do we have enough information to compute the answer? We sure do! We have 2 units of $10 or a total of $20 spent at the mall.

Step Seven: Write the answer in the sentence, and make sure the answer makes sense.

Marissa spent $20 at the mall.

Step Seven: Can you complete the answer now? Wonderful. "Marissa spent $20 at the mall." This makes perfect sense, doesn't it?

Milking the Problem for All It's Worth

- How much money did Marissa have at the beginning, before she went to the mall?

- How much more money did Marissa spend at the mall than she had left?

Teacher Note

In many of our math books and programs, we have this type of "work-backward" problem. The model method allows students to truly work backward with a visual tool, rather than solving the problem purely on an abstract level.

Fractions
(Subtraction)

A pie was cut into 6 equal pieces. Luke ate $\frac{1}{3}$ of the pie. How many pieces were left?

Step One: Read the entire problem.

"A pie was cut into 6 equal pieces. Luke ate $\frac{1}{3}$ of the pie. How many pieces were left?"

Step Two: Rewrite the question in sentence form, leaving a space for the answer.

There were ___ pieces left.

Step Three: Determine who and/or what is involved in the problem.

Pieces of pie

Step Four: Draw the unit bar(s).

Pieces of pie

Guided Conversation

Step One: Let's begin by reading the problem. Can you picture a pie cut into 6 pieces?

Step Two: Let's go to the question and rewrite it as a sentence. Good: "There were ___ pieces left."

Step Three: What is our next step? Yes, let's look at who is involved in this problem and what is involved in this problem. Until now, we have almost always written both who and what we are talking about in each word problem. In this problem, we're talking about Luke's pieces of pie, aren't we? But now that you have more experience with model drawing, we can handle things a little differently. Let's look at the question again. Do we need to know the name of the person eating the pie to find the answer? No, in this problem, we do not. We're really talking about just pieces of pie. Let's write that as our variable.

Step Four: Now draw the unit bar next to the variable. We're working with fractions, so make it long!

Step Five: Chunk the problem, adjust the unit bars, and fill in the question mark.

A

"A pie was cut into 6 equal pieces."

B

"Luke ate $\frac{1}{3}$ of the pie."

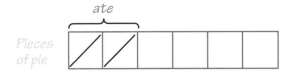

C

"How many pieces were left?"

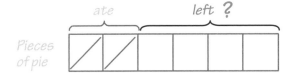

Step Five—A: The model is set up; let's go back and reread the problem. What is our first sentence or chunk of information? "A pie was cut into 6 equal pieces." How can we show this in our model? Divide the bar into 6 equal units, which represent slices? Correct! What fraction of the total pie is each slice? Absolutely! Each slice is $\frac{1}{6}$ of the total pie.

B: What do we learn from the next sentence? Yes, "Luke ate $\frac{1}{3}$ of the pie." Let's go back to the unit bar in our model. The unit bar is divided into $\frac{6}{6}$. What should we do to show that Luke ate $\frac{1}{3}$ of the pie? Good idea! We know that $\frac{2}{6}$ is the same as $\frac{1}{3}$. Let's put a brace over 2 of the units and label that part "ate." Those slices are now gone, because he ate them. How can we show this in the units? Put a slash through each one? Sure.

C: The next sentence is the question. Where should the question mark go in the model? Over the units that are left? Sounds good to me! Let's put a brace over those units, write the label "left" above them, and add the question mark. We're finished with this step!

Step Six: Correctly compute and solve the problem.

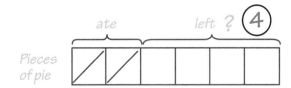

$6 - 2 = 4$

Step Seven: Write the answer in the sentence, and make sure the answer makes sense.

There were _4_ pieces left.

Step Six: Can you see how simple the solution is for this problem? How many slices are left? How many of you simply counted the units that are left? If you were to write a number sentence, what would you write? "6 – 2 = 4"? Sure!

Step Seven: There were 4 pieces left. It makes sense!

Milking the Problem for All It's Worth

- What fraction of the pie was left?
- If Luke had eaten $\frac{2}{3}$ of the pie, how many pieces would be left?

Teacher Note

Once they have some practice with model drawing, students learn to fine-tune the skill of identifying the variable. It's difficult at first, but as they progress along the learning continuum, students become more skilled at determining what's important and what's not.

Fractions
(Multiplication)

Cal had 2 oranges. He wanted to share $\frac{1}{4}$ of his oranges with his sister, Anna. What fraction of an orange did Cal give to Anna?

Step One: Read the entire problem.

"Cal had 2 oranges. He wanted to share $\frac{1}{4}$ of his oranges with his sister, Anna. What fraction of an orange did Cal give to Anna?"

Step Two: Rewrite the question in sentence form, leaving a space for the answer.

Cal gave _____ of an orange to Anna.

Step Three: Determine who and/or what is involved in the problem.

Cal's
oranges

Step Four: Draw the unit bar(s).

Cal's
oranges

Guided Conversation

Step One: Let's begin by carefully reading the problem. Can you picture 2 oranges? Now imagine that Cal wants to share $\frac{1}{4}$ of them with his sister. If Cal shares $\frac{1}{4}$ of his 2 oranges, will his sister get a whole orange or a part or fraction of an orange? Correct! She will get part or a fraction of 1 orange.

Step Two: Let's go to the question and rewrite it as a sentence, leaving a space for the answer. "Cal gave ___ of an orange to Anna."

Step Three: It's time to set up our model for this problem. Who and what are we talking about? Cal's oranges? Good. Let's write that to begin our model.

Step Four: What is the next step? Yes, draw a unit bar. Which word is a clue to draw a long unit bar? The word "fraction"? That's right!

Step Five: Chunk the problem, adjust the unit bars, and fill in the question mark.

A

"Cal had 2 oranges. He wanted to share $\frac{1}{4}$ of his oranges with his sister, Anna."

B

"What fraction of an orange did Cal give to Anna?"

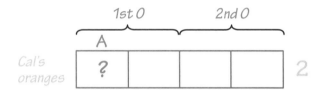

Step Five—A: Please reread the first sentence. What do we learn? Yes, we know that Cal had 2 oranges. Where should we write the "2" in our model? To the right of the unit bar? Yes, because that's Cal's total number of oranges. What does the next sentence tell us? Correct: Cal wanted to share part of his oranges, or $\frac{1}{4}$ of them, with his sister, Anna. Let's go to the unit bar. Think about this. For Cal to share $\frac{1}{4}$ of his oranges, he needed to divide his oranges into 4 equal parts. Let's divide our unit bar into 4 equal units to show this.

B: Now, out of the 4 parts, he wanted to give 1 part to Anna. Let's go back to the unit bar and write the label "A" for Anna above the first unit. Can you see that our model shows that Cal gave $\frac{1}{4}$ of his total oranges (units) to Anna? Great! Let's continue.

The next sentence is our question: "What fraction of an orange did Cal give to Anna?" If we go back to our unit bar, we can see that Cal gave $\frac{1}{4}$ of 2 oranges to Anna. Our question is "What fraction of an orange did Cal give to Anna?" How would we show each orange separately in our model? Good! Two units would represent each orange. Let's label the first 2 units "1st O" and the second 2 units "2nd O." Where should we put the question mark? Yes! Write it in the unit labeled "A" for Anna.

Step Six: Correctly compute and solve the problem.

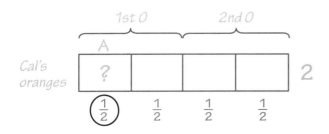

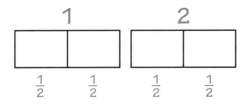

$\frac{1}{4}$ of $\frac{2}{1} = \frac{2}{4} = \frac{1}{2}$

Step Seven: Write the answer in the sentence, and make sure the answer makes sense.

Cal gave $\frac{1}{2}$ of an orange to Anna.

Step Six: It's time to solve the problem, and one way to solve it is to "read the model." To do this, let's add some more important labels. In the previous step, we identified the 2 separate oranges. Now let's look at 1 orange at a time. How many units are there for each orange? Good. There are 2 units for each orange. What can we call 1 of the 2 units? $\frac{1}{2}$? Great! Let's write the label "$\frac{1}{2}$" for each of the 4 units. Just to be sure, let's add them together: $\frac{1}{2} + \frac{1}{2} + \frac{1}{2} + \frac{1}{2} = 2$. Now you can see how and why we get $\frac{1}{2}$ when we find $\frac{1}{4}$ of 2. Now that we've added the labels, do you see how we can read the model to get the answer? Sure! Cal gave $\frac{1}{2}$ of an orange to Anna.

Step Seven: Let's add the answer to our sentence. "Cal gave $\frac{1}{2}$ of an orange to Anna." Check it out to be sure it makes sense!

Milking the Problem for All It's Worth

■ If Cal wanted to share $\frac{1}{2}$ of his oranges with Anna, how many oranges would he give to her?

■ What fraction of the oranges did Cal keep for himself?

Teacher Note

Too often, we simply teach our students procedures to find answers. This type of model-drawing problem builds and strengthens students' conceptual understanding of operating with fractions.

There is $\frac{1}{2}$ of a candy bar that needs to be divided evenly among 3 children. What fraction of the total candy bar will each child receive?

Step One: Read the entire problem.

"There is $\frac{1}{2}$ of a candy bar that needs to be divided evenly among 3 children. What fraction of the total candy bar will each child receive?"

Step Two: Rewrite the question in sentence form, leaving a space for the answer.

Each child will receive ___ of the candy bar.

Step Three: Determine who and/or what is involved in the problem.
Candy bar

Step Four: Draw the unit bar(s).

Candy bar

Step Five: Chunk the problem, adjust the unit bars, and fill in the question mark.

A
"There is $\frac{1}{2}$ of a candy bar . . ."

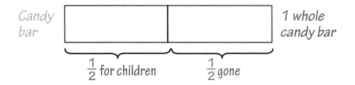

Guided Conversation

Step One: Let's begin by reading the problem. First, can you picture a whole candy bar? Now imagine that there is only $\frac{1}{2}$ of that candy bar and you need to divide that $\frac{1}{2}$ of a candy bar into 3 equal pieces. Does that help you see the problem we are solving?

Step Two: What's the next step? That's right! Rewrite the question as a sentence and leave a space for the answer. Can someone do that? Good. "Each child will receive ___ of the candy bar."

Step Three: What about our variable in this problem? How should we write it? Good. We're talking about the candy bar. Let's write that to begin our model.

Step Four: Next, we need to draw the unit bar. Since fractions are involved in this problem, let's draw a long unit bar.

Step Five—A: We can begin to model our problem. What does the first sentence tell us? "There is $\frac{1}{2}$ of a candy bar that needs to be divided evenly among 3 children"? Good. There's too much information, so let's model this sentence in chunks. First, "There is $\frac{1}{2}$ of a candy bar." Right now the unit bar represents 1 whole candy bar. Write "1 whole candy bar" to the right of the unit bar to show what the bar stands for. Now let's divide the unit bar into 2 equal parts and label one part "$\frac{1}{2}$ for children" and the other "$\frac{1}{2}$ gone." All set?

B

". . . that needs to be divided evenly among 3 children. What fraction of the total candy bar will each child receive?"

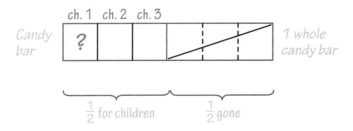

Step Six: Correctly compute and solve the problem.

A

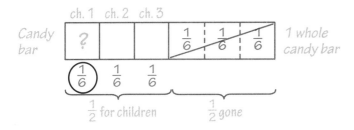

$$\frac{1}{2} \div 3$$
$$\frac{1}{2} \times \frac{1}{3} = \frac{1}{6}$$

B: Go to the $\frac{1}{2}$ of the candy bar that is gone. Do you remember how we mark the unit bar to show these parts are no longer there? Great! Draw a slash through the $\frac{1}{2}$ of the candy bar that is gone. Okay, let's return to finish the sentence: "that needs to be divided evenly among 3 children." Go to the $\frac{1}{2}$ of the unit bar for the children. We need to divide this $\frac{1}{2}$ into 3 equal parts or units. Let's label the first unit "ch. 1" for the first child and the other 2 units "ch. 2" and "ch. 3." To keep the units in our model the same or consistent, please also use dotted lines to divide the $\frac{1}{2}$ of the candy bar that is gone into 3 equal parts. Good! It's time to reread the final sentence or question. "What fraction of the total candy bar will each child receive?" Where should we write the question mark? Inside one of the first 3 units? Sure!

Step Six—A: I want you to study the model on your own or with a partner. Does the solution for this problem involve computation or using careful thinking to read the model? It can be solved either way, can't it? First we need to carefully analyze the information and read the model. How many equal units are there in the entire unit bar that represent 1 whole candy bar? A total of 6 units? Good. The question mark is in one of these units. What is the answer? Great work! Each child will receive $\frac{1}{6}$ of the total candy bar. I notice that someone set up the problem like this: "$\frac{1}{2} \div 3$." That student then inverted the second number in the math expression and multiplied. So he wrote, "$\frac{1}{2} \times \frac{1}{3} = \frac{1}{6}$." I know you can memorize this rule, but I want you to understand why it works. Using model drawing for our problem helps us understand.

B

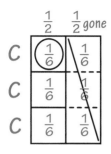

Step Seven: Write the answer in the sentence, and make sure the answer makes sense.

Each child will receive $\frac{1}{6}$ of the candy bar.

B: I also want to show you another model of this computation. Begin by drawing a rectangle. Vertically, divide the rectangle into 2 halves. Horizontally, divide the rectangle into 3 equal parts. We want to pay attention to only $\frac{1}{2}$ of the entire rectangle, so draw a slash through the other $\frac{1}{2}$ of the rectangle. Do you see our problem, "$\frac{1}{2} \div 3 = \frac{1}{6}$"? Again, you can see the entire rectangle contains 6 equal units, so each unit has a value of $\frac{1}{6}$. If you divide $\frac{1}{2}$ into 3 equal parts, each part or unit has a value of $\frac{1}{6}$.

Step Seven: Each child will receive $\frac{1}{6}$ of the candy bar. Is our answer reasonable? Yes, it is!

Milking the Problem for All It's Worth

■ What fraction of $\frac{2}{3}$ of the candy bar did 2 of the 3 children receive?

■ What fraction of $\frac{2}{3}$ of the candy bar did all 3 of the children receive?

Teacher Note

Too often, students simply memorize procedures and never conceptualize or understand the math they are using. The model method helps students understand dividing fractions with small, easy numbers, so when they are working with large, unwieldy numbers, they can use the procedure based on understanding, not mere memorization.

Fractions
(Mixed Operations)

Terra's monthly allowance is $48. She puts $\frac{1}{2}$ of her allowance into savings and gives $\frac{3}{4}$ of the remaining money to a local charity. How much money does Terra have left for herself each month?

Step One: Read the entire problem.

"Terra's monthly allowance is $48. She puts $\frac{1}{2}$ of her allowance into savings and gives $\frac{3}{4}$ of the remaining money to a local charity. How much money does Terra have left for herself each month?"

Step Two: Rewrite the question in sentence form, leaving a space for the answer.

Terra has $ ___ left for herself.

Step Three: Determine who and/or what is involved in the problem.

Terra's money

Step Four: Draw the unit bar(s).

Terra's money [ ]

Step Five: Chunk the problem, adjust the unit bars, and fill in the question mark.

A
"Terra's monthly allowance is $48."

Terra's money [ ] *$48*

Guided Conversation

Step One: Let's read this great problem and picture what it's about.

Step Two: Who can help us rewrite the question as a sentence, leaving a space for the answer? Good: "Terra has $___ left for herself."

Step Three: Who and what do we need to focus on for this problem? What is our variable? Terra's money? Good. Please write this to begin the model.

Step Four: What is our next step? Sure: let's draw a long unit bar, because we see that fractions are part of this problem.

Step Five—A: Are you ready to finish the model? Let's go back and reread the problem. What does the first sentence tell us? Yes, it tells us that Terra's monthly allowance is $48. Does this represent part of her monthly allowance or all of her monthly allowance? Good! It stands for her total monthly allowance, so let's put this amount to the right of the unit bar.

B

"She puts $\frac{1}{2}$ of her allowance into savings . . ."

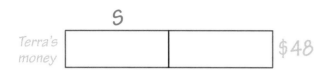

C

" . . . and gives $\frac{3}{4}$ of the remaining money to a local charity."

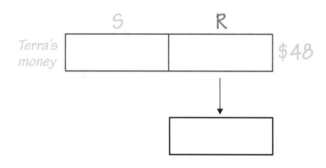

D

"How much money does Terra have left for herself each month?"

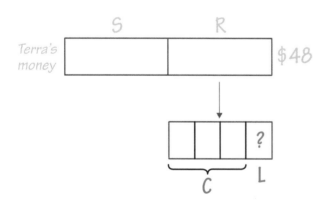

B: Let's move on to the next sentence. There's too much information, so let's model it in chunks. "She puts $\frac{1}{2}$ of her allowance into savings." How should we add this information to our model? Sure! We can divide the unit bar in $\frac{1}{2}$ and write the label "S" for savings over the first $\frac{1}{2}$ of the unit bar.

C: Let's go back to finish the sentence: "and gives $\frac{3}{4}$ of the remaining money to a local charity." Which part of the unit bar represents Terra's remaining money? The second $\frac{1}{2}$ of the unit bar? Great! Write the label "R" for remaining money over the second $\frac{1}{2}$ of the unit bar. Stop and think: did Terra give all or part of her remaining money to charity? Good: she gave only part of it. What part? That's right. She gave $\frac{3}{4}$ of her remaining money to charity. To model this, I want you to go to the unit bar and bring down and redraw just the second $\frac{1}{2}$ of the original unit bar—the "remaining" part. Draw an arrow from the original unit down to the redrawn unit. Now we can work with just Terra's remaining money.

D: What do we know? We know that Terra gave $\frac{3}{4}$ of her remaining money to charity. Let's divide our redrawn unit bar into 4 equal parts. To show that Terra gave $\frac{3}{4}$ of this remaining money to charity, let's draw a brace under 3 of the 4 units and label it "C" for charity. All set? It's time to finish the model by reading the question. "How much money does Terra have left for herself each month?" Where should the question mark go in the model? Which unit stands for the money Terra has left? Sure: the last or fourth unit in the redrawn bar stands for money Terra has left. Let's label that unit "L" for left for herself and put a question mark inside that unit. Great modeling!

Step Six: Correctly compute and solve the problem.

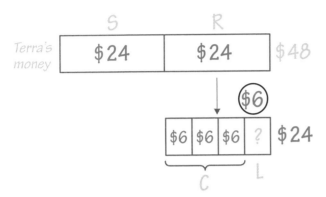

A. 2 u = $48
    1 u = $48 ÷ 2
    1 u = $24

B. 4 u = $24
    1 u = $24 ÷ 4
    1 u = $6

Step Seven: Write the answer in the sentence, and make sure the answer makes sense.

Terra has $6 left for herself.

Step Six: Where is a good place to begin to solve this problem? Very good! Let's go where we see a number. In the beginning unit bar, we see that 2 units equal $48. By dividing $48 by 2, we can see that each $\frac{1}{2}$ has a value of $24, right? Let's add this information to the model. How much money did Terra put into savings? Sure, $24. How much money was remaining? That's right: $24 was remaining. Let's continue to build on what we know. What was the total value of Terra's remaining money? Excellent: $24. Write that number to the right of the redrawn unit bar that stands for her remaining money.

   Again, we need to ask ourselves, "What do we know?" We now see that 4 units equal $24, so one unit is $24 divided by 4 or $6. Let's write "$6" above our question mark and circle it. Tell me about the values of the other 3 equal units? Sure. They each have a value of $6, too. Let's add that to the model. Excellent work!

Step Seven: Let's finish by adding the answer to our sentence and checking to be sure it makes sense. "Terra has $6 left for herself." Does it make sense? It sure does!

Teacher Note

In this type of problem—one with the word "remaining"—it helps students to bring down and isolate just a portion of the original unit bar.

Milking the Problem for All It's Worth

■ How much money did Terra donate to a local charity?

■ How much more money did Terra put in her savings than she gave to a charity?

Tiana spent $58.89 on clothes. She had $14.66 left. How much money did she have at first?

Step One: Read the entire problem.

"Tiana spent $58.89 on clothes. She had $14.66 left. How much money did she have at first?"

Step Two: Rewrite the question in sentence form, leaving a space for the answer.

Tiana had $ ___ at first.

Step Three: Determine who and/or what is involved in the problem.

Tiana's money

Step Four: Draw the unit bar(s).

Tiana's money

Step Five: Chunk the problem, adjust the unit bars, and fill in the question mark.

A

"Tiana spent $58.89 on clothes."

Tiana's money   C
$58.89

Guided Conversation

Step One: Let's begin by reading the problem. Can you picture what it's about? We know that Tiana spent part of her money on clothes and had part of her money left. We want to know how much she had at first.

Step Two: Next, we need to rewrite the question as a sentence. Let's leave a space for the answer. What can we write? Sure: "Tiana had $___ at first." This helps us focus on solving the problem.

Step Three: Who and what are we talking about in this particular problem? Tiana's money? Great! Let's begin our model.

Step Four: What should we do next? Great! Let's draw a unit bar that represents Tiana's money.

Step Five—A: Are you ready to fill in the model? What does the first sentence tell us? Sure. We learn that Tiana spent $58.89 on clothes. Did she spend all or part of her money on clothes? Part of her money? Yes. Let's write "$58.89" inside the unit bar and write a label "C" for clothes above it. Is there any more information in that sentence for our model? That's right: no.

B

"She had $14.66 left. How much money did she have at first?"

Step Six: Correctly compute and solve the problem.

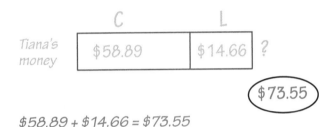

$58.89 + $14.66 = $73.55

Step Seven: Write the answer in the sentence, and make sure the answer makes sense.

Tiana had _$73.55_ at first.

B: Let's continue. "She had $14.66 left." Did she have part or all of her money left? Of course, it was part of her money. Write "$14.66" in the unit bar and add the label "L" for left above it. Let's divide the parts in our unit bar with a line. Which number is greater? Sure. Please show that $58.89 is the greater number by giving it more space inside the unit bar. What's our final step? Yes, add the question mark. Where should you write it? To the right of the unit bar, because we need to find the total amount of money Tiana had at first? Great!

Step Six: It's time to solve the problem. Please solve it on your own. I see that many of you added, because it's a part-whole problem. Wonderful!

Step Seven: Tiana had $73.55 at first. Does the answer make sense? Yes!

Milking the Problem for All It's Worth

- Tiana saw a pen for $8.79 and a notebook for $6.50. Will she have enough money left to buy both the pen and the notebook?

- How much more money would she need to be able to buy both the pen and the notebook?

- Tiana had $14.66 left after buying clothes. How much more money would she need to have $15?

Decimals
(Subtraction)

Sam wants to buy a book that costs $15.99. He has $8.43 right now. How much more money does Sam need to buy the book?

Step One: Read the entire problem.

"Sam wants to buy a book that costs $15.99. He has $8.43 right now. How much more money does Sam need to buy the book?"

Step Two: Rewrite the question in sentence form, leaving a space for the answer.

Sam needs $____ more to buy the book.

Step Three: Determine who and/or what is involved in the problem.

Sam's money

Step Four: Draw the unit bar(s).

Sam's money [   ]

Step Five: Chunk the problem, adjust the unit bars, and fill in the question mark.

A
"Sam wants to buy a book that costs $15.99."

Sam's money [   ] *$15.99*

Guided Conversation

Step One: Let's begin by reading the problem and picturing what it's about.

Step Two: Who can change the question to a sentence, leaving a space for the answer? Great: "Sam needs $___ more to buy the book." Let's write that down.

Step Three: The next step is to decide who and what we're talking about. Sam's money? Good. Let's write that to begin the model for this problem.

Step Four: Let's draw a unit bar in our model.

Step Five—A: Our model is set up. What's the next step? Reread the problem and add the information to the model? That's right! What do we learn from the first sentence? Yes: the total cost of the book Sam wants to buy is $15.99. Where should we write this total? To the right of the unit bar? Sounds good!

B

"He has $8.43 right now."

C

"How much more money does Sam need to buy the book?"

Step Six: Correctly compute and solve the problem.

$15.99 − $8.43 = $7.56

Step Seven: Write the answer in the sentence, and make sure the answer makes sense.

Sam needs $7.56 more to buy the book.

B: What is our next step? Yes: reread the next sentence, which tells us that Sam has part of the money he needs, or $8.43, right now. Where should we write this amount in our model? Good thinking! We'll write it inside our unit bar and add the label "has" above it.

C: It's time to reread the question. Does Sam need all or part of the money to buy the book? He already has $8.43 for the book, so we need to figure out how much more money he needs to reach a total of $15.99. Where should we write the question mark? Inside the unit bar? Excellent. Let's write the label "needs" over this part. Don't forget to separate the 2 values in the unit bar.

Step Six: Now that our model is finished, it's time to compute the answer. What kind of a problem do we have? Correct: we have a whole-part problem. Please find the answer on your own. Great work!

Step Seven: Let's add the answer to our sentence. "Sam needs $7.56 more to buy the book." Is this answer reasonable? It sure is! Now please go back to the unit bar in Step Five. Which value is greater? Yes, $8.43 is greater than $7.56. Can you check to see where you divided the 2 values in your unit bar? Is the part of your unit bar with "$8.43" slightly longer than the part with "$7.56"? Nice work!

Teacher Note

Revision is a great learning experience for students. Once you have completed a model-drawing problem, it's a good idea to have students go back and determine if any adjustments need to be made to the unit bar(s) and to the "who and what" or variable(s). Using pencils with erasers is recommended. Learning is a fluid process!

Milking the Problem for All It's Worth

- If Sam earns $5 more, how much more money will he still need to buy the book?

- If you round off the values to the closest dollar, approximately how much more money does Sam need to buy the book?

Decimals
(Multiplication)

An orange rope is 1.3 meters long. A green rope is 3 times as long as the orange rope. What is the combined length of the orange and green ropes?

Step One: Read the entire problem.

"An orange rope is 1.3 meters long. A green rope is 3 times as long as the orange rope. What is the combined length of the orange and green ropes?"

Step Two: Rewrite the question in sentence form, leaving a space for the answer.

The combined length of the orange and green ropes is ___ meters.

Step Three: Determine who and/or what is involved in the problem.

Length of orange rope

Length of green rope

Step Four: Draw the unit bar(s).

Length of orange rope ☐

Length of green rope ☐

Guided Conversation

Step One: Let's begin by reading the problem and picturing what it's about.

Step Two: We need to write our question as a sentence and leave a space for the answer. Let's write "The combined length of the orange and green ropes is ___ meters."

Step Three: Are we talking about any person in this word problem? No. We're talking about an orange rope and a green rope. What about the orange rope and green rope? We're talking about their lengths? Good. Let's write our 2 variables: "Length of orange rope" and "Length of green rope." Be sure to write one underneath the other and to leave space between them.

Step Four: What is our next step? Right! We need to give each variable a unit bar of equal size and value. Let's use the smaller, square unit bar for this problem. Tell me how the lengths of the 2 ropes appear right now in our model. Yes, they look the same, but we know that's not true. Let's go back and adjust our model by adding the facts.

Step Five: Chunk the problem, adjust the unit bars, and fill in the question mark.

A

"An orange rope is 1.3 meters long."

Length of orange rope | 1.3 m

Length of green rope | [ ]

B

"A green rope is 3 times as long as the orange rope. What is the combined length of the orange and green ropes?"

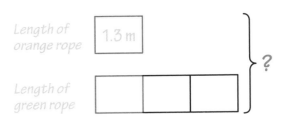

Step Five—A: It's time to reread the problem and add new information to make our model correct. What chunk of information does the first sentence give us? Right. "An orange rope is 1.3 meters long." Let's go to our model and write "1.3 m" inside the unit bar for the orange rope.

B: What's our next step? Reread the second sentence? Sure. "A green rope is 3 times as long as the orange rope." Let's again go to our model. How does the green rope compare to the orange rope right now? Yes, it looks the same. Let's make it correct. If we add 1 more equal unit, how many times as long is the green rope? Twice as long. Is this what the problem says? No, the problem says the green rope is 3 times as long. We need to add 1 more equal unit still. Let's make sure our model is correct. Do you see 1 unit next to the orange rope and 3 units next to the green rope? Great!

Let's move to the question: "What is the combined length of the orange and green ropes?" Where should we put the question mark? Yes, we need to draw a brace on the right side of our 2 variables and put the question mark to the right of the brace.

Step Six: Correctly compute and solve the problem.

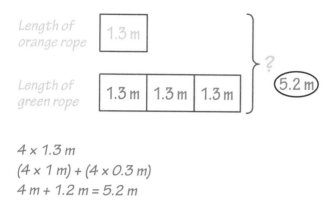

4 x 1.3 m
(4 x 1 m) + (4 x 0.3 m)
4 m + 1.2 m = 5.2 m

Step Seven: Write the answer in the sentence, and make sure the answer makes sense.

The combined length of the orange and green ropes is 5.2 meters.

Step Six: It's time for you to compute the answer, but there are units without values next to the green rope. Talk with a partner or think to yourself about the values for these units. Who will share? Great! The units in this model are the same size and have the same value. Since we know the value of the orange rope's unit is 1.3 meters, the value of each of the green rope's units must also be 1.3 meters. Let's add that information. When you're finished, please find the answer. I noticed someone solved the problem by using the distributive property. Great work!

Step Seven: Don't forget to add the answer to your sentence. "The combined length of the orange and green ropes is 5.2 meters." Make sure the answer is reasonable!

Milking the Problem for All It's Worth

■ How much longer is the green rope than the orange rope?

■ What fraction of the combined length of both ropes is the green rope? The orange rope?

Decimals
(Division)

Jiang needs to cut a ribbon into 3 equal pieces. If the ribbon is 2.4 meters long, what should be the length of each piece?

Step One: Read the entire problem.

"Jiang needs to cut a ribbon into 3 equal pieces. If the ribbon is 2.4 meters long, what should be the length of each piece?"

Step Two: Rewrite the question in sentence form, leaving a space for the answer.

Each piece of ribbon should be ___ meters long.

Step Three: Determine who and/or what is involved in the problem.

*Jiang's
ribbon*

Step Four: Draw the unit bar(s).

*Jiang's
ribbon*

Step Five: Chunk the problem, adjust the unit bars, and fill in the question mark.

A
"Jiang needs to cut a ribbon into 3 equal pieces."

*Jiang's
ribbon*

Guided Conversation

Step One: Let's first read the problem for understanding.

Step Two: Next, please rewrite the question as a sentence, leaving a space for the answer. We'll fill that in when we're finished solving the problem. Can someone rewrite the sentence? "Each piece of ribbon should be ___ meters long"? Perfect!

Step Three: In this problem, who and what are we talking about? Excellent. We're talking about Jiang's ribbon. Let's write that.

Step Four: What should we do next to set up our model for this problem? That's right. We need to draw a unit bar.

Step Five—A: It's time to reread the problem and add the information to our model. Who can read and tell us what we need to add from the first sentence? Good! We learn that Jiang needs to cut a ribbon into 3 equal pieces. How should we show this in our unit bar? Absolutely! Divide the unit bar into 3 equal units.

"If the ribbon is 2.4 meters long, what should be the length of each piece?"

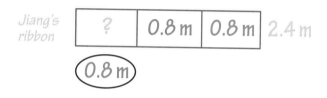

Jiang's ribbon | ? | | | 2.4 m

B: What should we do next? Yes, move on to the next sentence, which begins, "If the ribbon is 2.4 meters long." Let's stop with this chunk and add it to our model. Where should we write this length? Fine. Let's add it to the right of the unit bar, because 2.4 meters represents the total length of the ribbon. Please finish the question part of the last sentence. "What should be the length of each piece?" Where should we put the question mark? Great! We can put it in the first unit. We're trying to find the value of each unit.

Step Six: Correctly compute and solve the problem.

Jiang's ribbon | ? | 0.8 m | 0.8 m | 2.4 m

(0.8 m)

2.4 m ÷ 3 = 0.8 m

Step Six: I want each of you to use your model to do the computation. Good work with dividing decimals! Each ribbon should be 0.8 meters in length. Can you check your work by computing 3 × 0.8 meters?

Step Seven: Write the answer in the sentence, and make sure the answer makes sense.

Each piece of ribbon should be 0.8 meters long.

Step Seven: Each piece of ribbon should be 0.8 meters long. Is our answer reasonable? Sure. Now I'd like you to look back at the "who and what," or the variable for this problem, that we identified earlier. Now that we're finished, did we need Jiang's name in the variable? Is putting her name here incorrect? No! It's always a good idea to go back and make sure that the name we used for our variable makes sense! We learn by doing and checking.

Milking the Problem for All It's Worth

■ If Jiang cut the ribbon into 2 equal pieces, what would be the length of each piece?

■ If Jiang cut the ribbon into 6 equal pieces, what would be the length of each piece?

Ratio

The ratio of children to adults at the football game was 2 : 3. If there were 140 children at the football game, how many adults were there?

Step One: Read the entire problem.

"The ratio of children to adults at the football game was 2 : 3. If there were 140 children at the football game, how many adults were there?"

Step Two: Rewrite the question in sentence form, leaving a space for the answer.

There were ___ adults at the football game.

Step Three: Determine who and/or what is involved in the problem.

Children

Adults

Step Four: Draw the unit bar(s).

Children

Adults

Guided Conversation

Step One: Let's read the problem and picture what it's about. We've been studying ratios in class. What are we comparing in this problem? That's right! We're comparing the number of children to the number of adults attending a football game.

Step Two: Next we need to rewrite the question as a sentence and leave a space for the answer. Who can do that? Good. We'll write, "There were ___ adults at the football game."

Step Three: Who and what are we talking about in this particular problem? We're comparing children to adults. Let's begin our model by listing these 2 variables.

Step Four: Let's give each variable a unit bar of equal size and value. We'll use the small square unit bars for ratio problems. This will allow us plenty of space to show comparisons. What is the ratio right now in our model, before we add information? Yes, it's 1 : 1. We know that's incorrect, so let's continue.

Step Five: Chunk the problem, adjust the unit bars, and fill in the question mark.

A

"The ratio of children to adults at the football game was 2 : 3."

Children

Adults

B

"If there were 140 children at the football game, how many adults were there?"

Children   140

Adults   ?

Step Six: Correctly compute and solve the problem.

Children | 70 | 70 | 140

Adults | 70 | 70 | 70 | ? (210)

A. 2 u = 140
    1 u = 140 ÷ 2
    1 u = 70

B. 1 u = 70
    3 u = 3 × 70
    3 u = 210

Step Five—A: Are you ready to reread the first sentence? "The ratio of children to adults at the football game was 2 : 3." What is the symbol we use when writing ratios? Great! We use the colon. Let's make our model show the information in the problem. Right now the ratio in our model is 1 : 1. What should the ratio look like? Sure. We need 2 units for the children and 3 for the adults. Let's adjust the model so that it matches the language in the problem. Now we can see that the ratio of children to adults is 2 : 3.

B: Let's continue with the next sentence, "If there were 140 children at the football game, how many adults were there?" We need to focus on the first part of this sentence: "If there were 140 children at the football game." Where should we add this to our model? Very good. This number represents the total number of children, so we need to put it to the right of the children's unit bars. Let's finish the question: "how many adults were there?" Where should we put the question mark in the model? Sure: to the right of the adults' unit bars.

Step Six: It's time to solve the problem. Where do you see a number in our model? Yes, next to the children's unit bars. Look over the model. What do we know? Good! We know that 2 units equal 140, so 1 unit must have a value of 70. Be sure to add this information to the model. What can you tell me about the values of the units for the adults? Excellent! Each one has the same value as each of the units for the children. We can write "70" in each unit. Do you see how clear the computation is for this problem? We have 3 groups of 70 or 210 adults. Great work!

Step Seven: Write the answer in the sentence, and make sure the answer makes sense.

There were 210 adults at the football game.

Step Seven: There were 210 adults at the football game. Please check to be sure the answer makes sense!

Milking the Problem for All It's Worth

■ How many more adults than children were at the football game?

■ What fraction of the total number of people at the football game were adults?

■ What fraction were children?

If a photocopier can copy pages at the rate of 20 per minute, how many pages can it copy in $\frac{1}{2}$ hour?

Step One: Read the entire problem.

"If a photocopier can copy pages at the rate of 20 per minute, how many pages can it copy in $\frac{1}{2}$ hour?"

Step Two: Rewrite the question in sentence form, leaving a space for the answer.

The photocopier can copy ____ pages in $\frac{1}{2}$ hour.

Step Three: Determine who and/or what is involved in the problem.

Pages

Step Four: Draw the unit bar(s).

Pages [   ]

Step Five: Chunk the problem, adjust the unit bars, and fill in the question mark.

A

"If a photocopier can copy pages at the rate of 20 per minute, . . ."

min. 1
Pages [**20** |]

Guided Conversation

Step One: Let's read the problem and picture what it's about.

Step Two: Now we need to rewrite the question as a sentence and leave a space for the answer. What should we write? Sure: "The photocopier can copy ___ pages in $\frac{1}{2}$ hour."

Step Three: Are we talking about anyone in this problem? No, we're talking about the number of pages a photocopier can copy in $\frac{1}{2}$ hour. Let's begin the model by writing our variable: "Pages."

Step Four: Now we need to draw the unit bar that represents the number of pages.

Step Five—A: Let's go back and reread the problem. How many sentences are in this problem? Yes, there is only 1 sentence, and the second part of it is the question. What do we learn from the first part of the sentence? Good: we discover that a photocopier can copy pages at the rate of 20 per minute. Let's go to the unit bar and add this chunk of information. Begin by creating 1 unit at the far left of the bar and writing "20" inside the unit. Above it, write the label "min. 1."

B

" . . . how many pages can it copy in $\frac{1}{2}$ hour?"

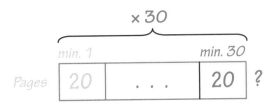

B: Now we need to finish the sentence, which includes the question: "how many pages can it copy in $\frac{1}{2}$ hour?" Before we can add this information to our model, what must we do? Good! Our model is in minutes and the question asks how many copies can be made in $\frac{1}{2}$ hour. We need to change hours to minutes. How many minutes are in $\frac{1}{2}$ hour? Sure! There are 30 minutes. Let's go back to the model. Does it make sense to draw 30 equal units? No, we already learned how to make a model using large numbers. We have the first unit showing 20 pages are copied in 1 minute. Now we can go to the far right end of the bar and draw another unit, putting "20" inside and writing the label "min. 30" above it. Between the first and last units, we draw an ellipsis, or 3 dots. Then let's add a brace and write " × 30" above it. We now have a model of 30 groups of 20.

And what is the question? "How many pages can it copy in $\frac{1}{2}$ hour?" Where should we write the question mark? Sure. We'll put it to the right of the unit bar, because we want to find the total number of copies the copier can make in this time period.

Step Six: Correctly compute and solve the problem.

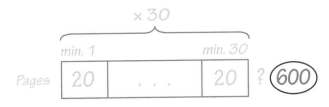

$30 \times 20 = 600$

Step Six: It's time to solve the problem. Do you see the computation here? The question is asking for 30 groups of 20, isn't it? What is the answer? 600 pages? Great! Let's add the answer to our sentence.

Step Seven: Write the answer in the sentence, and make sure the answer makes sense.

The photocopier can copy __600__ pages in $\frac{1}{2}$ hour.

Step Seven: The photocopier can copy 600 pages in $\frac{1}{2}$ hour. Is our answer reasonable? Yes!

Milking the Problem for All It's Worth

■ How many pages can it copy in 1 hour?

■ How many pages can it copy in $\frac{1}{4}$ hour?

Percentage

Sixty percent of the animals at the neighborhood pet store were dogs. If there were a total of 40 animals at the pet store, how many of the animals were dogs?

Guided Conversation

Step One: Read the entire problem.

"Sixty percent of the animals at the neighborhood pet store were dogs. If there were a total of 40 animals at the pet store, how many of the animals were dogs?"

Step One: Let's read the problem to get a picture of what it's about.

Step Two: Rewrite the question in sentence form, leaving a space for the answer.

There were ____ dogs at the pet store.

Step Two: Look at the final sentence. Find the part with the question: "how many of the animals were dogs?" How should we rewrite this question as a sentence? Sure. "There were ____ dogs at the pet store."

Step Three: Determine who and/or what is involved in the problem.

Animals

Step Three: What are we talking about in this problem? We're talking about animals, aren't we? Some of the animals are dogs, but our unit bar will represent all of the animals at the pet store, so begin the model with the label "Animals."

Step Four: Draw the unit bar(s).

Animals

Step Four: What should we do next to set up the model? Great! We need to draw a unit bar. Just as we drew a long unit bar for fractions, we need to do the same for decimals.

Step Five: Chunk the problem, adjust the unit bars, and fill in the question mark.

A

"Sixty percent of the animals at the neighborhood pet store were dogs."

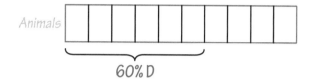

B

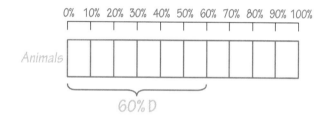

C

"If there were a total of 40 animals at the pet store, how many of the animals were dogs?"

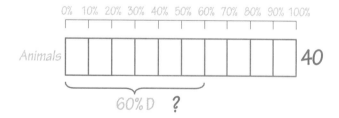

Step Five—A: Let's begin adding to the model of this problem by rereading the first sentence. What do we learn? The sentence tells us that part of the animals at the pet store, or 60% of them, were dogs. What does the word "percent" mean? Good. It means "parts per hundred." What else do you think of when we talk about percentages? Sure: fractions and decimals. If we wanted to use a fraction in place of "60%" in this problem, what would we write? Great! We could write that "$\frac{6}{10}$ of the animals at the pet store were dogs." We're building on what you already know with this problem! Let's go to the unit bar and divide it into 10 equal units. Below the first 6 units, draw a brace, and add the label "60% D."

B: When a word problem involves percentages, it helps to draw what is called a "percent ruler." Let me show you how to do this. Let's go to the unit bar. Each unit represents $\frac{1}{10}$ or 10% of the total. Above the unit bar, let's write the percentages in multiples of 10, starting with 0%, until we reach 100%.

Now take a minute to read the model. Can you see that $\frac{6}{10}$ is the same as 60%? Great! Were most of the animals at the neighborhood pet store dogs? Yes, our model clearly shows this.

C: Let's continue and reread the next sentence in the problem. The first part says "If there were a total of 40 animals at the pet store." There's a comma, so let's pause and go to the model to add this chunk of information. Where should we write the total of 40 animals? Sure: to the right of the unit bar. We still need to finish the question part of the last sentence: "how many of the animals were dogs?" We'll add the question mark next to the "D" label.

Step Six: Correctly compute and solve the problem.

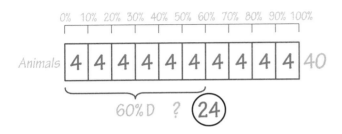

A. $10\,u = 40$
$1\,u = 40 \div 10$
$1\,u = 4$

B. $1\,u = 4$
$6\,u = 6 \times 4$
$6\,u = 24$

Step Seven: Write the answer in the sentence, and make sure the answer makes sense.

There were 24 dogs at the pet store.

Step Six: It's time to solve the problem. Where do you see a whole number in the problem? Good: "40" is to the right of the unit bar. What do we know? We can see that 10 units equal 40, so 1 unit equals 40 divided by 10, or 4. Each unit represents a value of 4 animals. Let's add this information to the model. Do you now see how simple the computation is? We just need to take 6 times 4 to determine that there were 24 dogs at the neighborhood pet store.

Step Seven: There were 24 dogs at the pet store. Is our answer reasonable? It sure is!

Teacher Note

When students are working on percent word problems, a percent ruler above the unit bar helps them see the connection between fractions and percentages.

Milking the Problem for All It's Worth

■ What percentage of the animals at the pet store were not dogs?

■ How many animals at the pet store were not dogs?

Bridge to Algebra

Together, Jasmine and Laura earned a total of $64 babysitting. If Jasmine earned $14 more than Laura, how much money did each girl earn?

Step One: Read the entire problem.

"Together, Jasmine and Laura earned a total of $64 babysitting. If Jasmine earned $14 more than Laura, how much money did each girl earn?"

Step Two: Rewrite the question in sentence form, leaving a space for the answer.

Jasmine earned $ ___ and Laura earned $ ___ babysitting.

Step Three: Determine who and/or what is involved in the problem.

Jasmine's money

Laura's money

Step Four: Draw the unit bar(s).

Jasmine's money [ ]

Laura's money [ ]

Guided Conversation

Step One: Let's read the problem and picture what it's about.

Step Two: What is the question in this problem? "How much money did each girl earn?" Let's rewrite the question into a sentence right now and leave a space for the answer. Who can do that? Good! We'll write, "Jasmine earned $___ and Laura earned $___ babysitting."

Step Three: Let's begin by identifying our variables. Who and what are we talking about in this problem? We're talking about Jasmine's money and we're also talking about Laura's money. Let's list both of those variables now.

Step Four: Remember, we need to give each variable a unit bar of equal size and value. Right now, in our model, it looks like the girls have the same amount of money. We know that's not true, so we'll go back and reread the problem and adjust the unit bars.

Step Five: Chunk the problem, adjust the unit bars, and fill in the question mark.

A

"Together, Jasmine and Laura earned a total of $64 babysitting."

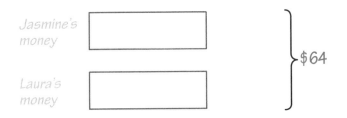

Step Five—A: The first sentence tells us that together, Jasmine and Laura earned a total of $64 babysitting. Let's go to the model and draw a brace to the right of Jasmine's and Laura's unit bars. To the right of the brace, let's write "$64." This is the total earned by both girls.

B

"If Jasmine earned $14 more than Laura, how much money did each girl earn?"

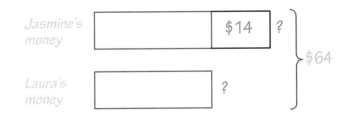

B: Now we need to return to the problem and reread the next sentence. There's a comma, so remember: that's where we'll pause and add new information to the model. "If Jasmine earned $14 more than Laura." Let's stop and go to the model. Right now it looks like Jasmine and Laura earned equal amounts. What did we just learn? That's right: we found out that Jasmine earned $14 more than Laura, so we need to go to Jasmine's unit bar and add another part. In that part, please write "$14." We've adjusted the unit bars to match the facts in the problem.

Let's continue with the final part of the last sentence, which is the question: "how much money did each girl earn?" How many question marks do we need to put in our model? Good! We need to put in 2 of them. Let's write a question mark to the right of each girl's unit bar. Good work!

Step Six: Correctly compute and solve the problem.

A. $64 - $14 = $50

B. 2 u = $50
   1 u = $50 ÷ 2
   1 u = $25

C. $25 + $14 = $39

Step Seven: Write the answer in the sentence, and make sure the answer makes sense.

Jasmine earned $39 and Laura earned $25 babysitting.

Step Six: It's time to solve this problem. What do we know? We know that the total both girls collected was $64, and that of that amount, $14 was earned by Jasmine. If we subtract $14 from $64, we find a difference of $50. Next, we can see that we have 2 equal units left, and if 2 units equal $50, then 1 unit has a value of $25. Let's add these values to the unit bars. It's obvious that Laura's total is $25, but what is Jasmine's total? Good: it's $25 + $14, or $39. It's wise to quickly check our computation. Do you see that (2 × $25) + $14 = $64? Our answer is right on the money!

Step Seven: Jasmine earned $39 and Laura earned $25 babysitting. That answer makes sense, doesn't it?

Algebraic Solution

Let:
x = Laura
Then:
x + $14 = Jasmine

Solve for x:
x + x + $14 = $64
2x + $14 = $64
2x = $50
x = $25

Laura (x) = $25
Jasmine (x + 14) = $39

Jasmine earned $39 and Laura earned $25 babysitting.

Milking the Problem for All It's Worth

■ If Jasmine earned only $8 more than Laura, how much money would each girl collect?

■ If Laura earned $12 less than Jasmine, how much money would each girl collect?

Bridge to Algebra

Maria rented 2 video games and 3 DVDs for a total of $23. Each video game cost $1.50 more to rent than each DVD. What was the cost of renting the DVDs?

Guided Conversation

Step One: Read the entire problem.

"Maria rented 2 video games and 3 DVDs for a total of $23. Each video game cost $1.50 more to rent than each DVD. What was the cost of renting the DVDs?"

Step One: Let's read the problem and picture what it's about.

Step Two: Rewrite the question in sentence form, leaving a space for the answer.

The cost of renting the DVDs was $ ___ .

Step Two: For the next step, we need to rewrite the question as a sentence and leave a space for the answer. What would be a good way to do that? Sure: "The cost of renting the DVDs was $___."

Step Three: Determine who and/or what is involved in the problem.

Cost of renting video games

Cost of renting DVDs

Step Three: What are our variables for this problem? What are we talking about? Good. We're talking about the cost of renting video games and the cost of renting DVDs. Let's begin our model by listing these variables.

Step Four: Draw the unit bar(s).

Cost of renting video games

Cost of renting DVDs

Step Four: What is our next step in setting up the model? Sure. We need to give each variable a unit bar of equal size and value. We'll use the square unit bars for this model. Let's begin by giving each variable 1 square unit. Each square unit will represent 1 video game or 1 DVD.

Step Five: Chunk the problem, adjust the unit bars, and fill in the question mark.

A

"Maria rented 2 video games . . ."

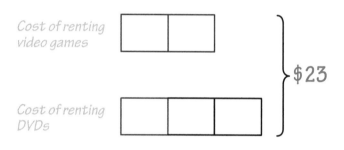

B

" . . . and 3 DVDs for a total of $23."

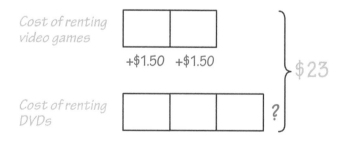

C

"Each video game cost $1.50 more to rent than each DVD. What was the cost of renting the DVDs?"

Step Five—A: Let's go back and reread the first sentence. "Maria rented 2 video games and 3 DVDs for a total of $23." There is too much information in one sentence, so let's add the facts to our model in chunks. We'll start with "Maria rented 2 video games." If we go to the model, it looks like she rented only 1 video game. Let's add another square unit. Now do you see 2 square units that represent 2 video games? Good.

B: Let's continue with the first sentence, "and 3 DVDs." Going back to our model, how many DVDs does it look like she rented right now? Yes. She has only 1 square unit, so it looks like she rented just 1 DVD. Go ahead and make it correct by adding 2 more square units, for a total of 3 units in her bar. All set? We're still not finished with the first sentence. We need to add "for a total of $23" to our model. Let's draw a brace to the right of both variables and add the total amount spent, or $23. There was a lot of information packed in that first sentence, wasn't there?

C: Moving on to the next sentence, we see that "Each video game cost $1.50 more to rent than each DVD." We want to keep our basic units the same size and value. To illustrate the additional money it cost to rent each video game, we need to add " + $1.50" below each video-game unit in the model.

The last sentence is the question. "What was the cost of renting the DVDs?" Where should we write the question mark in the model? Good! Let's put it to the right of the DVDs unit bar.

Step Six: Correctly compute and solve the problem.

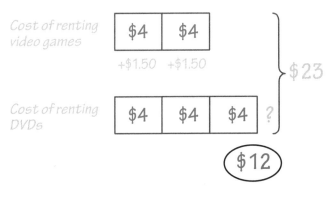

A. 2 x $1.50 = $3.00

B. $23.00 – $3.00 = $20.00

C. 5 u = $20.00
1 u = $20.00 ÷ 5
1 u = $4.00

D. 1 u = $4.00
3 u = 3 x $4.00
3 u = $12.00

Step Seven: Write the answer in the sentence, and make sure the answer makes sense.

The cost of renting the DVDs was $12.

Step Six: How should we solve this problem? Where should we start? What do we know? We know the total Maria spent renting all of the video games and DVDs. We also know the additional money required to rent the video games, so let's compute that total first. We have 2 groups of $1.50 for a total of $3. We now know that $3 of the $23 was spent on renting 2 video games. How much does that leave? That's right: $20. What's our next step? Sure. We know that each of our units has the same value. We have a total of 5 units (2 video games and 3 DVDs). If 5 units equal $20, then 1 unit equals $20 divided by 5. Each basic unit has a value of $4. Let's put the values in the units in our model. Do we have enough information to do the final arithmetic? Sure! We know that 3 × $4 = $12. Maria spent $12 renting the DVDs.

Step Seven: The cost of renting the DVDs was $12. Is our answer reasonable? Yes!

Algebraic Solution

Let:
x = cost of renting 1 DVD
Then:
x + $1.50 = cost of renting
1 video game

Solve for x:
2(x + $1.50) + 3x = $23.00
2x + $3.00 + 3x = $23.00
5x + $3.00 = $23.00
5x = $20.00
x = $4.00

The cost of renting the DVDs was $12.

Milking the Problem for All It's Worth

■ What was Maria's cost of renting the video games?

■ How much more did Maria spend on renting DVDs than on video games?

Problems for Independent Practice

PROBLEM 1

Addition
(Whole Numbers—Discrete Model)

There were 3 frogs sitting on a rock. Then 2 more frogs hopped onto the rock. How many total frogs were sitting on the rock?

PROBLEM 2

Addition
(Whole Numbers—Continuous Model)

Scrooge had 17 pennies in his piggy bank. He also had 8 dimes. How many total coins did Scrooge have in his piggy bank?

PROBLEM 3

Addition
(Whole Numbers with 3 Addends)

Elle read 54 pages of her book on Monday, 39 on Tuesday, and 24 on Wednesday. How many total pages did Elle read over the 3-day period?

PROBLEM 4

Subtraction
(Whole Numbers—Continuous Model)

Nancy went to the store with $25. She spent $13. How much money did she have left?

PROBLEM 5

Subtraction
(Whole Numbers—Continuous Model)

Kalil wants to buy a video game that costs $32. He has $17. How much more money does Kalil need to buy the video game?

PROBLEM 6

Subtraction
(Whole Numbers—Comparison)

At the lunch stand, 128 chicken and 117 beef tacos were sold. How many more chicken tacos were sold than beef tacos?

PROBLEM 7

Mixed Operations
(Whole Numbers—Addition & Subtraction)

There are 124 cars, 25 motorcycles, and some trucks in a parking lot. If there are 205 total vehicles in the lot, how many trucks are there?

PROBLEM 8

Multiplication
(Whole Numbers—Single-Digit Factor)

There are 5 vases on the table and 4 flowers in each vase. How many total flowers are in the vases?

PROBLEM 9

Multiplication
(Whole Numbers—Comparison)

There are tulips, daisies, and daffodils growing in a garden. There are 2 times as many daisies as tulips and 3 times as many daffodils as tulips. If there are 12 daisies, how many total flowers are in the garden?

PROBLEM 10

Division
(Whole Numbers—Partitive)

Jamil packed 54 oranges into 6 bags. If he put the same number in each bag, how many oranges did he put in 1 bag?

PROBLEM 11

Division
(Whole Numbers—Partitive)

The custodian needs to set up 156 chairs for an assembly. If he puts them in 12 rows, how many chairs should he put in each row?

PROBLEM 12

Division
(Whole Numbers with Remainder—Quotitive or Measurement)

Jerry made 38 muffins. He needs to put all of the muffins into boxes. Each box holds 6 muffins. How many boxes will Jerry need?

PROBLEM 13

Mixed Operations
(Whole Numbers—Multiplication & Addition)

Carter mailed 6 packages. The first 3 packages weighed 2 pounds each, the next 2 packages weighed 1 pound each, and the last package weighed 3 pounds. What was the total weight of all 6 packages?

PROBLEM 14

Mixed Operations
(Whole Numbers—Multiplication & Subtraction)

Caitlin had 156 beads. She gave 32 beads to each of her 3 friends. How many beads did Caitlin have left?

PROBLEM 15

Fractions
(Addition)

Jia earned money babysitting. She spent $\frac{1}{4}$ of the money on lunch. She spent $\frac{1}{2}$ of the money on a DVD, and she saved $4. How much money did Jia spend on the DVD?

PROBLEM 16

Fractions
(Subtraction)

A pizza was cut into 5 equal slices. Fred ate $\frac{3}{5}$ of the pizza. How many slices were left?

PROBLEM 17

Fractions
(Multiplication)

Kim found 6 plates of pizza left after her party. There was $\frac{1}{2}$ of a pizza on each plate. Kim put the pizza halves together. How many whole pizzas did Kim have left?

PROBLEM 18

Fractions
(Division)

There was $\frac{1}{2}$ of a chocolate cake left over after dinner. Four people shared it equally the next day. What fraction of the whole chocolate cake did each person eat?

PROBLEM 19

Fractions
(Mixed Operations)

Angela baked cookies. She gave $\frac{1}{3}$ of them to her sister, and she put $\frac{5}{8}$ of the remaining cookies in the freezer. If she had 1 dozen cookies left, how many cookies did she bake?

PROBLEM 20

Fractions
(Mixed Operations)

Marcus wrote 3 pages of his science report on Monday. He wrote $\frac{2}{3}$ of the remainder on Tuesday. He still needed to write 2 more pages. How many total pages was Marcus's science report?

PROBLEM 21

Decimals
(Addition)

A pine tree is 4 meters tall. An apple tree is 2.5 meters taller than the pine tree. What is the total combined height of both trees?

PROBLEM 22

Decimals
(Subtraction)

Doug walked 2.3 kilometers for a local fundraiser. Chad walked 1.8 kilometers. How many more kilometers did Doug walk than Chad?

PROBLEM 23

Decimals
(Multiplication)

A farmer sold 30 dozen eggs at $1.50 a dozen. How much total money did the farmer receive for his eggs?

PROBLEM 24

Decimals
(Division)

If 24.75 kilograms of flour need to be divided evenly among 5 bags, how many kilograms of flour should be put in each bag?

PROBLEM 25

Decimals
(Mixed Operations)

Miguel spent $4.95 on a hamburger, $2.59 on fries, and $2.12 on a milkshake. He gave the clerk a $10 bill. How much change did Miguel receive?

Ratio

Eric and Tyrone shared $72 in the ratio of 3 : 5. What was Eric's share of the money?

Ratio

Scott was making punch for a picnic. He mixed pineapple juice with ginger ale in the ratio of 3 : 2. If Scott used 6 quarts of pineapple juice, how much punch did he make for the picnic?

Ratio

The ratio of almonds to sunflower seeds to raisins in a bag of trail mix is 2 : 5 : 3. If there are 10 ounces of sunflower seeds in the bag, what is the total weight of the bag of trail mix?

Ratio

The ratio of trucks to cars in the parking lot is 2 : 5. If there are 40 cars in the parking lot, how many trucks are there?

Ratio

There are pens, pencils, and markers in a desk drawer. The ratio of pens to pencils is 2 : 3. The ratio of markers to pencils is 1 : 3. If there are 4 pens in the drawer, how many more pencils than markers are there?

PROBLEM 31

Rate

If Bill saves $45 a week from his paycheck, how much will he save in 12 weeks?

PROBLEM 32

Rate

A worker can pack 72 boxes of oranges in 2 hours. At this rate, how many boxes of oranges can she pack in 8 hours?

PROBLEM 33

Rate

The cost of admission to a concert is $35 per adult and $22 per child. What will be the admission price for 3 adults and 2 children?

PROBLEM 34

Rate

The cost of a taxi ride is $2.50 for the first mile and $0.75 for each additional mile. Carrie took a taxi from the airport to the hotel and paid $11.50 for the fare, before the tip. What was the distance from the airport to the hotel?

PROBLEM 35

Rate

A photocopier can print 40 sheets of paper per minute. If there are 500 sheets of paper in a ream, how long will it take the photocopier to print 2 reams of paper?

PROBLEM 36 · Percentage

There were 30 questions on a science test. Mr. Newton correctly answered 90% of the questions. How many questions did Mr. Newton answer correctly?

PROBLEM 37 · Percentage

Brad was shooting baskets at the park. He successfully made 60% of his shots. If he made 36 baskets, how many shots did he miss?

PROBLEM 38 · Percentage

There are a total of 40 puppies, kittens, and birds in a pet store. Of all those animals, 60% are puppies, 30% are kittens, and the rest are birds. How many kittens are in the pet store?

PROBLEM 39 · Percentage

Rachel's monthly salary for her after-school job is $400. She puts 35% of her salary into her savings account each month. How much does Rachel put into her savings each month?

PROBLEM 40 · Percentage

There are 220 rooms in an office building. Out of all the rooms, 90% are air-conditioned. How many more rooms are there that are air-conditioned than rooms that are not?

PROBLEM 41

Bridge to Algebra

Alma and Elmo sold a total of 96 raffle tickets for a school fundraiser. Alma sold 14 more tickets than Elmo. How many tickets did each student sell?

PROBLEM 42

Bridge to Algebra

Mrs. I. M. Sweet bought 5 ice cream cones and 3 banana splits for the girls in her chess club. Each banana split cost $1.25 more than each ice cream cone. If Mrs. Sweet spent $9.75 on the banana splits, how much did the 5 ice cream cones cost?

PROBLEM 43

Bridge to Algebra

If $\frac{2}{3}$ of a number is 4, what is the number?

Solution Keys

1

Frogs 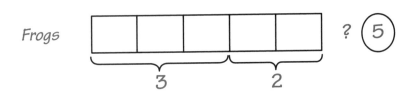 ? (5)

3 + 2 = 5

There were a total of _5_ frogs sitting on the rock.

2

Scrooge's coins

P	D
17	8

? (25)

17 + 8 = 25

Scrooge had a total of _25_ coins in his piggy bank.

3

Elle's pages

M	T	W
54	39	24

? (117)

54 + 39 + 24 = 117

Elle read a total of _117_ pages over the 3-day period.

4

Nancy's money

spent	left
$13	? ($12)

$25

$25 – $13 = $12

Nancy had _$12_ left.

5

has   needs

Kalil's money | $17 | ? | $32

$15

$32 – $17 = $15

Kalil needs $15 more to buy the video game.

6

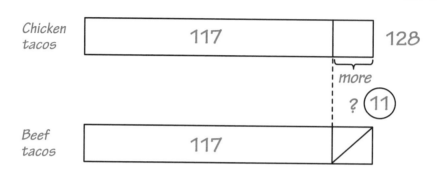

Chicken tacos   117   128

more

?   11

Beef tacos   117

128 – 117 = 11

There were 11 more chicken tacos sold than beef tacos.

7

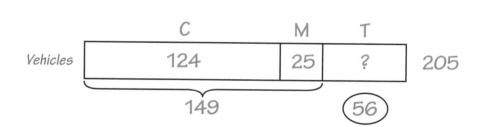

C   M   T

Vehicles | 124 | 25 | ? | 205

149   56

A.   124 + 25 = 149

B.   205 – 149 = 56

There are 56 trucks in the parking lot.

8

Flowers
V V V V V
| 4 | 4 | 4 | 4 | 4 | ? ⟨20⟩

5 × 4 = 20

There are <u>20</u> total flowers in the vases.

9

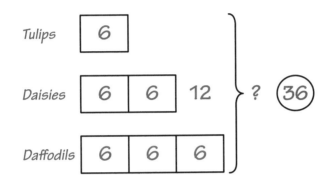

A. 2 u = 12
    1 u = 12 ÷ 2
    1 u = 6

B. 1 u = 6
    6 u = 6 × 6
    6 u = 36

There are <u>36</u> total flowers in the garden.

10

Jamil's oranges
B B B B B B
| ? | 9 | 9 | 9 | 9 | 9 | 54
⟨9⟩

6 u = 54
1 u = 54 ÷ 6
1 u = 9

Jamil put <u>9</u> oranges in each bag.

11

Chairs

1st row   12th row

?   . . .   13   156

⑬

$156 \div 12$

$(144 \div 12) + (12 \div 12)$

$12 + 1 = 13$

The custodian should put _13_ chairs in each row.

12

Jerry's muffins

B B B B B B B

6 6 6 6 6 6 2   38

⑦ ? # of boxes

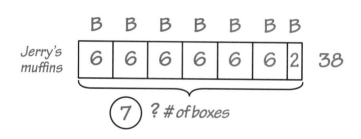

38	
− 6	− 1 box (1)
32	
− 6	− 1 box (2)
26	
− 6	− 1 box (3)
20	
− 6	− 1 box (4)
14	
− 6	− 1 box (5)
8	
− 6	− 1 box (6)
2	− 1 box (7)

Jerry will need _7_ boxes. (He will fill 6 boxes and have 2 muffins in the seventh box.)

13

Packages' weight

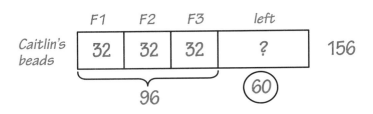

$(3 \times 2 \text{ lb.}) + (2 \times 1 \text{ lb.}) + 3 \text{ lb.}$
$6 \text{ lb.} + 2 \text{ lb.} + 3 \text{ lb.} = 11 \text{ lb.}$

The total weight of all 6 packages was __11__ pounds.

14

Caitlin's beads

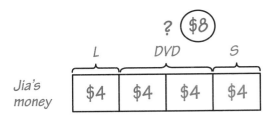

A. $3 \times 32 = 96$
B. $156 - 96 = 60$

Caitlin had __60__ beads left.

15

Jia's money

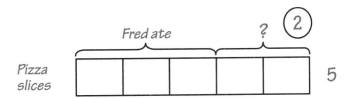

$\$4 + \$4 = \$8$

Jia spent __$8__ on the DVD.

16

Pizza slices

There were __2__ slices of pizza left.

17

Kim's pizza

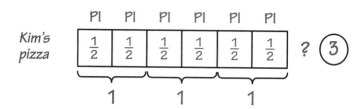

$6 \times \frac{1}{2} = \frac{6}{2}$

$\frac{6}{2} = 3$

Kim had _3_ whole pizzas left after her party.

18

Chocolate cake

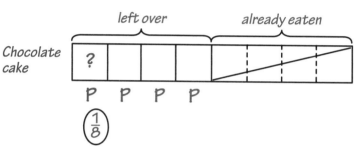

$\frac{1}{4}$ of $\frac{1}{2} = \frac{1}{8}$

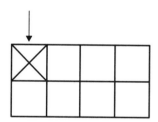

Each person ate $\frac{1}{8}$ of the whole chocolate cake.

19

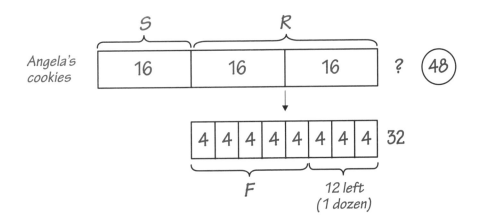

Angela's cookies

A. $3\,u = 12$

    $(1\,doz. = 12)$

    $1\,u = 12 \div 3$

    $1\,u = 4$

B. $1\,u = 4$

    $8\,u = 8 \times 4$

    $8\,u = 32$

C. $2\,u = 32$

    $1\,u = 32 \div 2$

    $1\,u = 16$

D. $1\,u = 16$

    $3\,u = 3 \times 16$

    $(3 \times 10) + (3 \times 6)$

    $30 + 18 = 48$

    $3\,u = 48$

Angela baked _4 dozen (48)_ cookies.

20

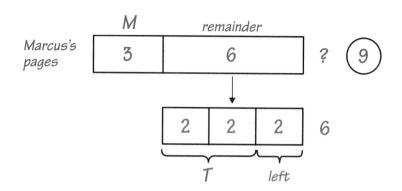

A. $1 u = 2$
    $3 u = 3 \times 2$
    $3 u = 6$

B. $3 + 6 = 9$

Marcus's science report was _9_ total pages.

21

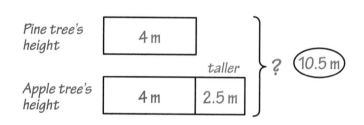

$4 m + 4 m + 2.5 m = 10.5 m$

The total combined height of both trees is _10.5_ meters.

22

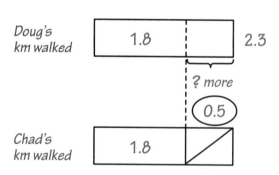

$2.3 km - 1.8 km = 0.5 km$

Doug walked _0.5_ more kilometers than Chad.

23

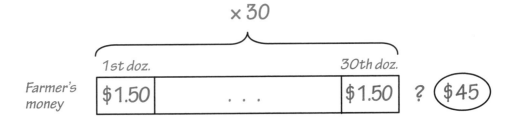

Farmer's money

1st doz.		30th doz.
$1.50	. . .	$1.50

? $45

30 x $1.50 = $45.00

The farmer received a total of $45 for his eggs.

24

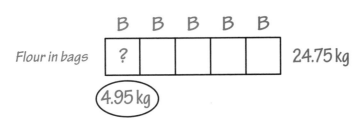

Flour in bags

B B B B B

?				

24.75 kg

4.95 kg

5 u = 24.75 kg
1 u = 24.75 kg ÷ 5
1 u = 4.95 kg

There should be 4.95 kilograms of flour in each bag.

25

Miguel's money

H   F   M   C $0.34

$4.95	$2.59	$2.12	?	$10

$9.66

A. $4.95 + $2.59 + $2.12 = $9.66

B. $10.00 – $9.66 = $0.34

Miguel received $0.34 in change.

26

Eric's money

| $9 | $9 | $9 | ? | $27 |

Tyrone's money

| $9 | $9 | $9 | $9 | $9 |

} $72

A. $8u = \$72$
    $1u = \$72 \div 8$
    $1u = \$9$

B. $1u = \$9$
    $3u = 3 \times \$9$
    $3u = \$27$

Eric's share of the money was $27.

27

Pineapple juice (qt.)

| 2 | 2 | 2 | 6

Ginger ale (qt.)

| 2 | 2 | 4

} ? (10 qt. or $2\frac{1}{2}$ gal.)

A. $3u = 6$ qt.
    $1u = 6$ qt. $\div 3$
    $1u = 2$ qt.

B. 6 qt. $+ 4$ qt. $= 10$ qt.

OR

6 qt. + 4 qt.
2 qt.   2 qt.
8 qt.   2 qt.
2 gal. $\frac{1}{2}$ gal.

Scott made 10 quarts or $2\frac{1}{2}$ gallons of punch for the picnic.

28

| Almonds (oz.) | 2 | 2 | 4 |

Sunflower seeds (oz.): 2 2 2 2 2 10

Raisins (oz.): 2 2 2 6

} ? 20 oz. or 1 lb. 4 oz.

A. 5 u = 10 oz.
   1 u = 10 oz. ÷ 5
   1 u = 2 oz.

B.
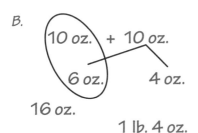
10 oz. + 10 oz.
6 oz.   4 oz.
16 oz.
1 lb. 4 oz.

The total weight of the bag of trail mix is _20 ounces or 1 pound 4 ounces._

29

Trucks: 8 8 ? 16

Cars: 8 8 8 8 8 40

A. 5 u = 40
   1 u = 40 ÷ 5
   1 u = 8

B. 2 × 8 = 16

There are _16_ trucks in the parking lot.

30

Pens	2	2	4

Pencils
| 2 | 2 | 2 |

Markers
| 2 | ? ④ |

A. 2 u = 4
   1 u = 4 ÷ 2
   1 u = 2

B. 2 x 2 = 4

There are _4_ more pencils than markers in the desk drawer.

31

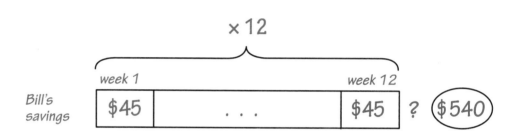

× 12

week 1   week 12

Bill's savings
| $45 | . . . | $45 | ? ($540) |

12 x $45
(12 x $40) + (12 x $5)
$480 + $60 = $540

Bill will save _$540_ in 12 weeks.

32

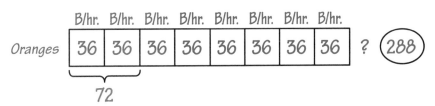

Oranges

72

A. 2 u = 72
   1 u = 72 ÷ 2
   (70 ÷ 2) + (2 ÷ 2)
   35 + 1 = 36
   1 u = 36

B. 1 u = 36
   8 u = 8 × 36
   (8 × 30) + (8 × 6)
   240 + 48 = 288
   8 u = 288

The worker can pack _288_ boxes of oranges in 8 hours.

33

Cost of admission

adults   children

(3 × $35) + (2 × $22)
$105 + $44 = $149

The admission price for 3 adults and 2 children will be _$149_.

34

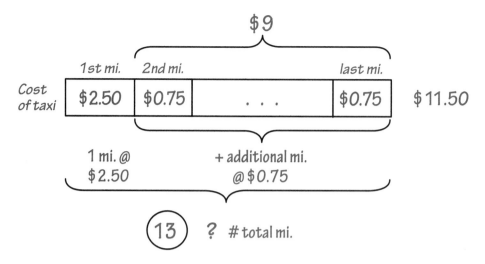

A. $11.50 - $2.50 = $9.00

B. $9.00 ÷ $0.75 = 12.0 mi.

C. 1 mi. + 12 mi. = 13 mi.

The distance from the airport to the hotel was 13 miles.

35

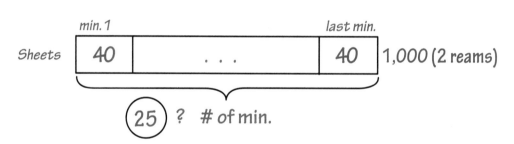

2 × 500 = 1,000
1,000 ÷ 40
100 ÷ 4 = 25 min.

It will take 25 minutes to print 2 reams of paper.

36

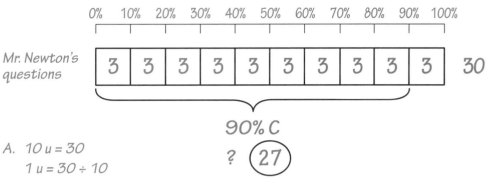

Mr. Newton's questions

A. 10 u = 30
    1 u = 30 ÷ 10
    1 u = 3

B. 9 × 3 = 27

Mr. Newton correctly answered _27_ questions on the science test.

37

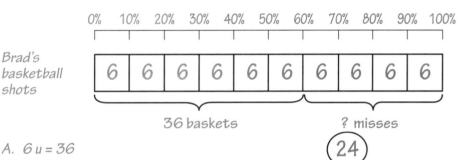

Brad's basketball shots

A. 6 u = 36
    1 u = 36 ÷ 6
    1 u = 6

B. 4 × 6 = 24

Brad missed _24_ of his shots.

38

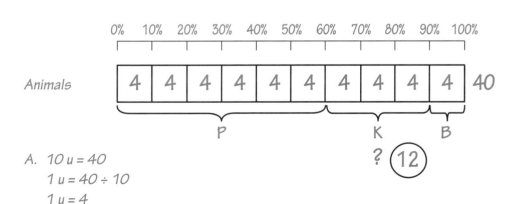

Animals

A. 10 u = 40
    1 u = 40 ÷ 10
    1 u = 4

B. 3 × 4 = 12

There are _12_ kittens in the pet store.

39

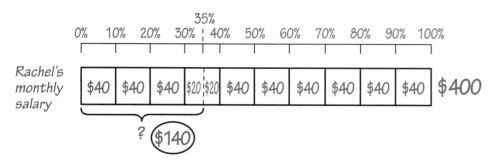

A. 10 u = $400
    1 u = $400 ÷ 10
    1 u = $40

B. 35% is equivalent to 3.5 units.

C. (3 x $40) + $20
    $120 + $20 = $140

Rachel puts $140 into her savings each month.

40

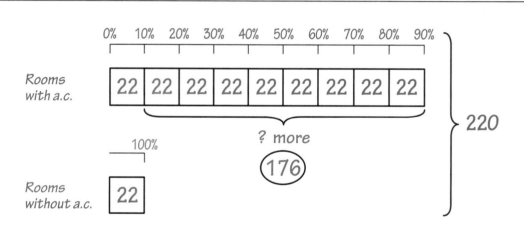

A. 10 u = 220
    1 u = 220 ÷ 10
    1 u = 22

B. 8 x 22
    (8 x 20) + (8 x 2)
    160 + 16 = 176

There are 176 more air-conditioned rooms than rooms that are not air-conditioned.

41 Model-Drawing Solution

| Alma's tickets | 41 | 14 | ? |
| Elmo's tickets | 41 | ? | 41 |

55

96

A. $96 - 14 = 82$

B. $2u = 82$
    $1u = 82 \div 2$
    $1u = 41$

C. $41 + 14 = 55$

Alma sold 55 tickets and Elmo sold 41 tickets.

Algebraic Solution

A. *Let:*
    x = Elmo's tickets
    $x + 14$ = Alma's tickets

B. *Solve for x:*
    $x + x + 14 = 96$
    $2x + 14 = 96$
    $2x = 82$
    $x = 41$

C. Elmo's tickets (x) = 41
    Alma's tickets (x + 14) = 55

Alma sold 55 tickets and Elmo sold 41 tickets.

Model-Drawing Solution

Cost of
ice cream cones

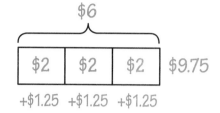

Cost of
banana splits

A. $3 \times \$1.25 = \$3.75$

B. $\$9.75 - \$3.75 = \$6.00$

C. $3u = \$6.00$
$1u = \$6.00 \div 3$
$1u = \$2.00$

D. $5 \times \$2.00 = \$10.00$

The 5 ice cream cones cost $\underline{\$10}$.

Algebraic Solution

A. Let:
x = cost of 1 ice cream cone
$x + \$1.25$ = cost of 1 banana split

B. Solve for x:
$3(x + \$1.25) = \$9.75$
$3x + \$3.75 = \$9.75$
$3x = \$6.00$
$x = \$2.00$

C. Solve for cost of ice cream cones (5x)
$5 \times \$2.00 = \$10.00$

The 5 ice cream cones cost $\underline{\$10}$.

Model-Drawing Solution

Number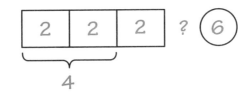

A. $2\,u = 4$
   $1\,u = 4 \div 2$
   $1\,u = 2$

B. $3 \times 2 = 6$

The number is 6 .

Algebraic Solution

A. Let:
   x = number

B. Solve for x:
   $\frac{2}{3}x = 4$
   $2x = 12$
   $x = 6$

The number is 6 .

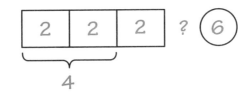

References & Resources

References

Chen, Sandra. 2008. *The parent connection for Singapore math.* Peterborough, NH: Crystal Springs Books.

———. 2009. *Word problems for model drawing practice,* Level 4. Peterborough, NH: Crystal Springs Books.

Forsten, Char. 1996. *Teaching thinking and problem solving in math.* New York: Scholastic.

———. 2008. *Solving word problems.* CD-ROM. Peterborough, NH: Crystal Springs Books.

———, and Torri Richards. 2009. *Math talk.* Peterborough, NH: Crystal Springs Books.

Hazekamp, Jana. 2009. *Word problems for model drawing practice,* Level 2 and Level 3. Peterborough, NH: Crystal Springs Books.

———, and Catherine Jones Kuhns. 2009. *Word problems for model drawing practice solution key,* Levels 1 and 2. Peterborough, NH: Crystal Springs Books.

———, and Sandra Chen. 2009. *Word problems for model drawing practice solution key,* Levels 3 and 4. Peterborough, NH: Crystal Springs Books.

Kuhns, Catherine Jones. 2009. *Building number sense.* Peterborough, NH: Crystal Springs Books.

———. 2009. *Word problems for model drawing practice,* Level 1 and Level 5. Peterborough, NH: Crystal Springs Books.

———, and Anni Stipek. 2009. *Word problems for model drawing practice solution key,* Levels 5 and 6. Peterborough, NH: Crystal Springs Books.

Lee, Joseph D. 2004. *Primary mathematics: Challenging word problems,* U.S. Edition (Grades 1–6). Singapore: SNP Panpac.

Lee, Peng Yee, Ed. 2009. *Teaching primary school mathematics.* Singapore: McGraw-Hill.

Ministry of Education, Singapore. 2009. *The Singapore model method for learning mathematics.* Singapore: Panpac Education.

Ng Chye Huat, Juliana and Lim Kian Huat. 2001. *A handbook for mathematics teachers in primary schools.* Singapore: Federal Publications.

Parker, Thomas H., and Scott J. Baldridge. 2004. *Elementary mathematics for teachers.* Okemos, MI: Sefton-Ash Publishing.

Polya, G. 2004. *How to solve it.* Princeton, NJ: Princeton University Press.

Primary mathematics textbooks, standards edition: 1A, 1B, 2A, 2B, 3A, 3B, 4A, 4B, 5A, and 5B. 2007. Singapore: Marshall Cavendish.

Principles and standards for school mathematics. 2000. Reston, VA: National Council of Teachers of Mathematics.

Singapore Ministry of Education. 2003. *Primary mathematics textbooks, U.S. edition: 1A, 1B, 2A, 2B, 3A, 3B, 4A, 4B, 5A, 5B, 6A, and 6B.* Singapore: Marshall Cavendish.

Stipek, Anni. 2009. *Word problems for model drawing practice,* Level 6. Peterborough, NH: Crystal Springs Books.

Helpful Websites

Crystal Springs Books: www.SDE.com/crystalsprings
Model-drawing workbooks, professional books, and manipulatives

Great Source: www.greatsource.com
Math in Focus series

National Council of Teachers of Mathematics: www.nctm.org
Lists of curriculum standards and focal points

SingaporeMath.com Inc.: www.singaporemath.com
Primary Mathematics U.S. Edition and Standards Edition textbooks, workbooks, and teacher guides; Singapore Math information, curriculum descriptions, Web links, and other resources

The Singapore Maths Teacher: www.thesingaporemaths.com
Help for teachers learning model drawing

Staff Development for Educators: www.SDE.com
Singapore Math information, resources, links, placement tests; conferences, seminars, and online courses for professional development

Thinking Blocks: www.thinkingblocks.com
Free, interactive website for learning and practicing model drawing

Index

Char Forsten is also the author or coauthor of:

Differentiated Instruction
Differentiating Textbooks
Hyperactive Students Are Never Absent
If You're Riding a Horse and It Dies, Get Off
Just One More Thing!
Math Strategies You Can Count On
Math Talk
The More Ways You Teach, the More Students You Reach
Question-Answer Relationships
Solving Word Problems (CD-ROM)
Teaching Thinking and Problem Solving in Math
The Top 13 Warning Signs That It's Time to Retire
Volunteers Are Vital
You Know You're a Teacher If . . .